Letters to My Son:

Advice for Today's Pastors and Christian Leaders

By

Daryl Ward

Published by

Queen V Publishing
Englewood, Ohio
QueenVPublishing.com

Published by

Queen V Publishing
Englewood, Ohio
QueenVPublishing.com

Copyright © 2019 by Daryl Ward

All rights reserved. No part of this book may be reproduced or transmitted in any form or by any means, electronic or mechanical, without prior written consent of the author, except for the inclusion of brief quotes in a review.

Unless otherwise noted, Scriptures are from the New King James Version of the Holy Bible.

Library of Congress Control Number: 2019912860

ISBN-13: 978-0-9962991-3-8

Cover design by Candace K

Co-written with Chet Kelly Robinson

Edited by Valerie J. Lewis Coleman of PenOfTheWriter.com

Printed in the United States of America

Dedication

I dedicate this book to my parents:

Lester and Maudie Ward

Acknowledgments

My wife, Vanessa Oliver Ward,
the wind beneath my wings.

Chet Robinson, who took my rough notes and crafted a voice that was mine.

The Omega Baptist Church family, who loved and nurtured the five different pastors I matured into over this wonderful 30-year journey.

Anyone who encouraged, inspired or mentored me on this pastoral journey.

Table of Contents

Foreword by Reverend Vanessa Ward 11
Foreword by Reverend Dr. Otis Moss, Jr. 13
Preface 15
Introduction 17
Letter 1 Prayer is Your Fuel 23
Letter 2 Administration: A Recipe for Success 35
Letter 3 Worship! 49
Letter 4 Preparing Your Sermon 63
Letter 5 Preaching 73
Letter 6 Partnering with Your Spouse 87
Letter 7 Your Support System: Family and Friends 103
Letter 8 Time Management 117
Letter 9 Protect Yourself: Morality and Integrity 129
Letter 10 Walking in Faith 141
Letter 11 Transitions: Knowing When It's Time to Go 153
Closing Thoughts 167
About Reverend Daryl Ward 171
About Chet Kelly Robinson 172
About Queen V Publishing 173

Letters to My Son

Foreword by Reverend Vanessa Ward

When I first read this manuscript, so many emotions filled me. I rejoiced, I cried, I laughed and I marveled at the faithfulness of God at work in Daryl Ward's life. While I am honored to be his wife of 37 years, I am more grateful to God for blessing our ministry. I have not observed from the seat of spectator, but I am privileged to participate as co-laborer, confidante and best friend. We have shared the joys, disappointments and triumphs of ministry…together!

I was elated when Daryl mentioned writing this book. I whole-heartedly agreed that he should share his years of faithful service and the courage it took to pioneer transformative initiatives. I encouraged him to bear witness of his physical healing, and God's decision to bless his ministry beyond a life-threatening illness. While many pastors may have comparable experiences, few can rival Daryl's uncanny ability to simplify the intricacies of pastoral leadership into practical and approachable advice, thus paving the way for the next generation of leaders. He is genuine and vulnerable in sharing his experiences and reflections. He imparts what God blessed him to receive to our son, Joshua Daniel Ward, a gifted and humble young man who will succeed him as the next senior pastor of Omega Baptist Church.

Letters to My Son exposes Daryl's heart for ministry and his love for God and God's people. That includes his abiding love for his biological son and daughters, as well as many spiritual ones. I pray that churches and ministries will be refreshed and energized as young and emerging pastors apply Daryl's divinely inspired advice. This book speaks not only to our son, but to the next generation of God's leaders, providing necessary courage and ingenuity to guide and serve in such times as these.

Reverend Vanessa Oliver Ward

Foreword by Reverend Dr. Otis Moss, Jr.

The ministries of Rev. Daryl Ward, Esq., Rev. Vanessa Ward, Ph.D. (ABD), and successor, Pastor Joshua Ward, Esq., are unique, excellent and miraculous. The Wards, Omega Baptist Church, United Theological Seminary, their ministries and path of succession make for a phenomenal narrative. Their works represent a chapter in prophetic ministry, leadership and service. They must be studied in the academy, utilized in organizational behavior, consulted in institutional transitions and used in prayer, meditation and spiritual practice.

This book is beautiful in content and what it represents is a miracle in our time. Therefore, the catalogue of experiences cannot be copied or duplicated. This teaching narrative is a powerful spiritual autobiography. However, the power is not given for copycat duplication, but creative inspiration and application with excellence and integrity.

Rev. Daryl Ward has given us a document of dedication that deals with ministry, suffering, sacrifice, service and transition. Throughout *Letters To My Son: Advice for Today's Pastors and Christian Leaders*, we hear and feel "the sound of the genuine" (Howard Thurman). The sound comes from God through Daryl Ward and his multiple experiences as a sacred gift to us and coming generations. Thank you, Rev. Ward, and thanks be to God.

As I end this brief and inadequate foreword, I must comment on the witness behind the document.

Rev. Ward and Dr. Lenard Sweet led one of the most dynamic chapters in the history of theological/seminary education at United Theological Seminary. They brought together the best family of difference makers including scholars, writers, activists, mentors and mentees, servant leaders, transformational and prophetic people. *Letters to My Son: Advice for Today's Pastors and Christian Leaders* is a testimony and testament to that brief and glorious moment of revolutionary theological education. The moment pointed the way, in Daryl Ward's words: "From vision to victory." This book is inseparably related to that unique and dynamic moment.

Reverend Dr. Otis Moss, Jr.

Preface

While each letter of this book is addressed "Dear Son" because Joshua was foremost on my mind, the content is intended for every pastor or Christian leader.

I worked with my co-writer to organize these letters around topics at the core of the hills and valleys I faced while leading my church. Designed to provide a new perspective and proven advice for what ails you, I encourage you to use this book as a collection of "just-in-time" entries to reference as needed.

Letters to My Son can help you view leadership through different lenses and be inspired with insights you can discuss with your spouse, church staff, associate ministers and ministry mentors.

In the context of Hebrews 12:1, think of me as one of the contemporary "cloud of witnesses" God uses to give insight for your leadership journey.

I would be honored to hear how *Letters to My Son* served your ministry experiences. Please do not hesitate to contact me at darylward01@gmail.com.

Reverend Daryl Ward

Daryl Ward

Introduction

Dear Joshua,

This book began as a series of letters to you, my only son. The Omega Baptist Church congregation had just voted you in as pastor-elect, installing you over a body of believers I have been honored to lead for over three decades. While I was moved by the inescapable pride of a father watching his son earn the trust of people united in service to our Lord, as a pastor, I found myself asking, "What's next?" I knew God had not brought us this far to sit back and welcome hundreds of worshippers each week. How could we continue to influence the City of Dayton?

God has worked mightily through our church, teaching us how to serve Him with distinction when the offering plate was full and when it was light, when our sanctuary burst at the seams and when we were dismayed by the empty rows. We saw our membership grow from 100 to over 4,000 at its peak, managed annual budgets as large as $2,000,000 and established a citywide reputation as one of the most-innovative churches focused on urban evangelism and discipleship.

We earned that reputation with lots of hard labor, prayer and resilience. We spent years developing leaders who founded and evolved over 40 community-focused ministries in areas including social justice, preventative health, global missions and evangelism. Your mother administered the Omega School of Excellence, a charter school that elevated urban youths' academic performance and positioned them for high school and collegiate success. Our bi-annual Youth Explosion services drew 4,000 teens a year. We introduced hundreds of un-churched youth to Christ, and provided a spiritual home where they received regular discipleship. Not only did we have a television ministry that reached a viewership of nearly 500,000, I was blessed to host a weekly social justice and political talk radio show on one of Dayton's most-popular radio stations. Perhaps we earned our reputation as "church unusual" hosting thousands of worshippers at citywide Easter services at the University of Dayton Arena.

One reason I was confident in your readiness to lead, was that you stood with us through a "winter" season. As Dayton weathered one economic blow after another, Omega experienced the effect in our membership, tithes and offerings. Simultaneously, a devastating illness sidelined me for months, contributing to a further decline in membership and narrowing of ministry beyond the four walls of the church.

We have not always made perfect decisions, but we did our best to follow God's voice as we walked through the wilderness. As your mother stepped in to lead the church, God restored my health and inspired us to find our way toward the light. By the time your readiness to lead was fully apparent, our membership had rebounded, the financial foundation stabled and influence expanded. The Hope Center for Families, which will empower low-income individuals and families with life skills, work skills and character to break the bonds of poverty will hopefully be completed.

Despite my confidence in the church's health as you step into the role of lead pastor, I felt a need to document the lessons I have learned across decades in ministry. I read books like Thom S. Rainer and Eric Geiger's *Simple Church* and Rick Warren's *The Purpose-Driven Church*. I found them helpful because they laid out the wisdom behind the methodologies those pastors used to identify and pursue their churches' God-given purpose. In the same way those books formed my leadership of Omega, I hope to provide touchstones to help you plot the church's next chapter.

As I jotted notes, I could not shake a sense that my initial scope—an audience of one—was too limited. I have more free time than I have had in a long time, which allowed me to reflect on the spiritual gifts God revealed in me. One of my more-evident gifts has been an ability to connect with people through personal testimonies of God's work in my life. This gift first surfaced when I began seminary studies at Colgate Rochester Divinity School in New York. It didn't take long for me to get an interim placement as director of student recruitment, apparently because of the way I connected with potential seminarians using the story of my calling to ministry.

Joshua, many of your fellow pastors and Christian leaders did not grow up with your advantages—nor mine. Your upbringing in a home where both parents are highly-educated pastors was not the norm; especially among African-Americans. While my home environment was modest, I had an advantage that is uncommon for far too many of your brothers and sisters in ministry: a loving, dedicated father. From my earliest memories, through his untimely death when I was a relatively young man, Lester Ward never let me doubt that he was fully invested in seeing me achieve my potential.

As I ministered to our congregation, community and brothers and sisters in ministry, I am aware of many ministry leaders who did not share this type of parental support. In addition to the guidance received from my parents, God blessed me with a wealth of powerful mentors.

My life from that moment has been supernatural in so many ways. I think the kids today would say, "It's been 'extra.'" I was not born into a preacher's family; I have no ties to a legacy of preaching nobility. Despite that, God gifted me to be in conversation and relationship with many eminent, nationally recognized people of the African American church and with leaders and pioneers from across this nation. My tenure as president and COO of United Theological Seminary, where I helped establish an African-American Ministries program, landed me on the cover of national magazines and put me into relationship with such luminaries as Cornel West, Michael Eric Dyson, Andrew Young, Otis Moss, Jr. and Samuel Proctor. God equipped me with spiritual mentors who helped me without expecting anything in return.

I use this book to return the favor. I pray these letters will resonate in the hearts and minds of many younger, and in some cases newly-minted, pastors and leaders who can benefit from what God revealed to me through others.

Every so often, I am amidst pastors who stun me with the way they carry themselves when they think no parishioners are watching. I assume you see the same phenomenon in your travels and networking. Perhaps some of these carnal pastors have no business being in ministry, at least not until they allow major transformation in their souls.

For many, however, I sense the problem is that they are misguided...called, but not led. How many of them had the benefit of sincere, Holy Spirit-filled role models at home or in ministry? I pray that this book can play a small part in closing this critical leadership gap.

Apostle Paul used the timeless tool of letter writing to advise the leaders of churches he founded on how to govern congregations and advance their ministries. Not only did he leverage letters to churches in Galatia, Phillipi and Ephesus, he mentored Timothy in the same manner. That example inspires me as I present this straightforward advice designed to speak to the daily challenges faced when leading churches, ministries or other Christian organizations.

Daryl Ward

Letter 1

Prayer is Your Fuel

Principle:

Pray without ceasing.
—1 Thessalonians 5:17

If I could share only one piece of advice it would be never stop praying. Your prayer life is the focal point of your journey as a pastor and leader. Use it to keep in constant communication with God about everything.

Dear Son,

You may be thinking, "I know, I know." The importance of prayer may sound too obvious, but don't tune me out just yet. Let's examine why a rich prayer life is so essential for you as a leader. Investing now in authentic, transparent communication with God will pay dividends throughout your ministry and your walk with God. And as I learned, payoffs come in ways you could never have predicted.

If I Had Not Prayed, I Would Have Been Lost

December 2004 was a dynamic time in the life of our church and my family. The church purchased the 30-acre campus of a local seminary, spurring ambitious development plans, challenging fund-raising goals and increased engagement with civic leaders and associations. Your mother had matured into her ministry calling, not only earning seminary degrees and delivering passionate sermons, but also administering the Omega School of Excellence Charter School. Our partnership seemingly had the church positioned to continue its reputation as the largest, most-progressive African-American body of believers in metro Dayton.

The morning of December 28th; however, my life changed without warning. Dayton had experienced heavy snowstorms and temperatures in the low twenties. I left home ready to navigate the icy roads to attend a church staff meeting. I was frustrated to see that the roads were in much worse shape than stated on the news. I slid off the road at least two times, colliding with snow banks that required me to shovel the car free.

Vanessa had called my cell phone to see why I was late for the meeting. I was tight-lipped, answering questions with one-word answers. My breathing was heavy, and I was unable to explain why the car kept running off the road.

Arriving at church, I grumbled to myself that no one had warned me about the roads. Striding into the staff meeting, I was unaware that instead of my usual attire of a sweater and dress slacks, I wore an old pair of sweats and a ratty pair of sneakers. I did not look well-groomed.

Given my tardiness, appearance and odd behavior, Vanessa rushed me to our family physician, Dr. Morris

Brown. His initial review of my disoriented behavior and physical symptoms indicated that I had potentially suffered a mild stroke. He insisted on further testing at a hospital.

I have no memories of most of this day, nor many of those that followed. I lost all motor functions on my left side. I could not feed myself or even digest pureed foods. Rendered mute, I came perilously close to death several times. This arduous day was the first of a nearly three-year journey that tested the very foundation of our family, limits of our spiritual faith, and loyalty of our church family. Vanessa was forced to oversee my care while keeping Omega afloat with unwavering leadership and inspired preaching. Our lives—and the ministry of Omega Church—would never be the same.

I faced challenges few humans could help me through. But as has been the case in too many situations for me to count, investment in my prayer life made the difference in delivering me from a seemingly insurmountable trial. A dynamic prayer life benefits people far beyond you; it empowers you to better serve both your congregation and your community.

While I pray that you never experience a health crisis as severe as mine, rest assured that you and your church or Christian organization will face unforeseen detours that test resiliency. A daily commitment to your prayer life—an effort that may at times feel unnecessary or gets in the way of "the urgent"—can make the difference between life and death; both spiritual and physical.

Let's consider some of those urgent obstacles that can obstruct your prayer life, and the benefits of overcoming them.

Overcoming Obstacles

Pastors face all types of barriers to an effective prayer life. Church administrative meetings, community activities, sermon preparation, academic study, television and apps on your smart phone are just the beginning of distractions. When I consider the frenzy of activity that filled my days before I fell ill, I wonder, "Did I really do all that?" While I managed twenty-five associate ministers and staff, over forty active ministries, a prison outreach program, a full-service bookstore, a community development corporation, and a charter school, I felt the church's focus on socially relevant ministry required me to touch as many corners of the Dayton community as possible. I spent each day running between church meetings, pow-wows with city, county and state politicians, and board of trustee meetings for countless area universities, charities, arts organizations and seminaries.

As God blesses the prosperity of your ministry, you will be tempted by the noise of these types of activities and more. My counsel: address these "prayer blockers" using this three-step process:

1. Seek God regularly to help you evaluate the many activities crowding your calendar. Ask Him to reveal which ones are not in alignment with His vision for your ministry (the *Administration Letter* on page 35 delves further into this lesson). As He reveals the answer, prune those from your schedule.
2. Pray for discernment to identify remaining activities aligned with your vision, but can be delegated to a staff member or associate minister.

3. Use the time freed by implementing the first two steps to set a committed daily hour to be still and seek God in prayer. This time is for you to commune with God as a believer; not as a preacher preparing a sermon, or a leader seeking God's tactical guidance. This time is for you to invest in your friendship with God, and develop an ear for His voice.

Why Prayer is Not a Luxury

Prayer played a vital role in my ministry long before my illness, and continues to do so. Staying in constant communication with God helps me perform all aspects of pastoring more effectively. Prayer keeps me in touch with the Holy Spirit in a way that best overcomes my human frailties. It reminds me that I am an ambassador of Christ in every environment and every interaction.

Prayer will help you maintain focus, and manage your ambassadorship to bring God glory. I often participate in high-stakes board meetings and other community events where some might expect me to do most of the talking. When God gives me something important to contribute, I speak up, but I find that when you listen to God, at times, He leads you to silence.

Have you been in situations where, because a certain respected or ill-reputed person is there, others behave differently than they would otherwise? As a minister of the gospel, you can positively influence people when you have a prayer-filled, Holy Spirit-fueled level of discretion. I have endured meetings with fellow Christian leaders who believed they needed to live up to their title. They filled the air with the sound of their voice, which took conversations off track or injected inaccurate, unhelpful statements.

You don't have to go out like that! A healthy prayer life can help you communicate with confidence that you are staying true to God's purpose for you, your church and its ministry. Think of it as a down payment that will deliver a return on investment at pivotal points in your ministry. During those moments where you must choose between God-ordained options and those orchestrated by man, a rich prayer life is one of the best investments for the health of your ministry.

What Does a Healthy Prayer Life Look Like?
Prayer is not a ritualized action where you fold your hands in solitude to recite Matthew 6:9-13. Prayer is direct communication with God that feeds the "God space" in your heart. The connection allows you to sense God is doing something great at your most lonely, disheartened moments despite appearances.

I best describe my prayer life and habits in three periods: the early prime of my ministry, during the worst days of my health crisis and in the final phase of my service as Omega's senior pastor. Although each period was distinct, my reliance on prayer was a consistent factor.

As I worked to establish Omega as a "church unusual," I often met resistance from constituencies within the church and throughout the community. Investing daily in my connection with God gave me peace throughout tumultuous times, kept me from faltering in the face of opposition and halted my attempts to override what God was doing with meager efforts to "fix things."

As Omega became an increasingly popular church known for attracting members from traditional houses of worship, we experienced blowback. In the face of hostile actions, multiple people offered advice that equated to "If you let them treat you like that, you're a punk." I cannot say that I didn't consider such advice, but investment in prayer led me to focus on God's voice telling me some version of "Be at peace; be still." The ability to hold to "peace that passes all understanding" played a major role in the course that Omega charted as a growing congregation committed to serving and empowering the local community.

Thank God, my prayer life was vibrant and rich before I fell ill! I was diagnosed with lesions on my brain, the likely result of a virus that attacked my brain stem. After nearly dying in a Dayton hospital and being transported to the Cleveland Clinic, where the exact nature of my affliction was identified, I spent over 100 days bedridden. I barely spoke, swallowed or willed my hands and feet to do simple tasks.

My prayer life during this time was simple. I could not verbalize prayers, but I heard them in my head. "God bless me. God help me. God take care of my family." Nothing deep or impressive, but without question, my advance prayers and connection with God allowed me to depend on Him amidst what seemed a devastating circumstance.

While hospitalized, my ability to speak slowly returned. Two speech pathologists challenged me to prepare and deliver a sermon for them in a week. When one arrived to hear my message and settled at my bedside, I left her speechless with my sophisticated message. I cannot quote my exact words, but I know that it was a message of two or three sentences best summed up as, "God is good."

Her eyes narrowed and brows wrinkled; I assume in confusion. Her reply was memorable. "Is that it?"

I was hurt. I had gone as deep and as involved as was possible for me at that time. Thank God, again, for that prayer connection and peace. I understood that while I had a long trek to be the pre-illness preacher, God would accompany me throughout the journey. That abiding sense of God's presence carried me throughout my hospital stay. It gave me peace and emboldened me to participate in decisions about my treatment, even in some cases exerting my will over Vanessa's and my doctors' expressed preferences. As appreciative as I was for their respective roles in my recovery, my prayer connection provided an additional source of guidance concerning the best way forward.

Prayer Made the Difference...and Still Does

As you absorb from my testimony, think on the following prayer-life prescriptions that can help deepen your daily, by-the-minute connection with God:

- Build your prayers on the best foundation available — the same Scriptures that you study as a teacher and preacher.

  In the spring of 2005, weeks after the miraculous recovery that allowed me to leave the hospital, I realized that I was in for a much longer test of my connection with God. Returning to the pulpit to deliver my first sermon in months, I was no longer the articulate, witty preacher my congregants had known for nearly two decades. Unable to walk under my own power, I relied on a wheelchair. Two deacons helped me climb the few steps leading to the pulpit. Holding steady to a walker as I delivered my sermon, I struggled to read the notes and my words did not come easily. I stuttered so badly that I wondered whether anyone could get edification from my words. When the service ended, I endured awkward conversations with congregants unable to hide the doubt and fear in their eyes. Although Vanessa had done a wonderful job leading the church in my absence, we were already hearing of members who had written me off and transferred to other churches.

With a lengthy, uncertain rehabilitation ahead of me, my prayer life consisted of ongoing, relentless communication with God about the ways in which I drew encouragement and inspiration from scriptural accounts of healing and faith. The Gospels were a rich source of reminders of God's power to move in my circumstances, and this passage was especially impactful:

Jesus replied, "I tell you the truth, if you have faith and do not doubt, not only can you do what was done to the fig tree, but also you can say to this mountain, 'Go, throw yourself into the sea,' and it will be done. If you believe, you will receive whatever you ask for in prayer."
—Matthew 21:21-23

Meditating and praying on Scriptures like this affirmed my trust in God's ability and willingness to move mountains on my behalf. This blessed assurance kept me going even as Omega's membership fluctuated. I leaned on the leadership of Vanessa and other church ministers and officials. Every time the daily realities of life threatened to overwhelm me, the spiritual perspective fed by constant prayer and meditation on applicable Scriptures provided the emotional boosts I needed.

- Be authentic in your prayers—express the full range of your emotions.

  While I had always practiced it in my own way, this principle was revealed most-clearly from Vanessa's example. Several years after my full recovery, as we reflected on the experience, I read the journal Vanessa kept during my hospitalization. I was struck by the transparent, authentic prayers she recorded each day. It was clear that she went to God and spoke as a trusting, but pained, daughter addressing a loving Father whose counsel she needed. Every emotion coursing through her was shared with God including fear, bewilderment, longing and grief.

  Through it all, Vanessa clung and returned to the faithful belief that God would work out my healing and restore us as man and wife. I believe that these ongoing conversations with God fed Vanessa's ability to not only stand by me and our family, but to also lead the church and preach almost every Sunday for three months. No matter what the day held, she processed it through frank, expressive, healing talks with the Father.

- Walk in the power of intercessory prayer—for your congregation and yourself.

  Separate letters address the important ways in which shepherds must intercede for their congregations, but when it comes to the "self-care" of developing a healthy prayer life, account for the benefits received from others' intercessory prayer.

While I give due credit to the medical providers, therapists and other professionals who God used to heal me, I place as much significance in the prayers others delivered on my behalf. People across the world prayed for me, but a major source of the unexplainable optimism that passed over me during the darkest days was the organized, fasting-powered prayers of my congregation.

Reverend Arnita Peavy, one of our most-fiery and beloved associate ministers, led a church-wide program of prayer and fasting devoted to my healing. On a daily basis, she and dozens of others gathered before God on my behalf. The prayer ministry assigned each member a prayer partner with whom they could remotely pray on a regular basis, lifting up not only Vanessa and me, but the entire congregation. Leaning on Scriptures for inspiration, and their experience of God's presence, they continued for months and then years as I slowly regained faculties I had lost. God honored their faithful toil. My complete healing was not coincidental. This experience drove home the wisdom of James 5:16:

Therefore confess your sins to each other and pray for each other so that you may be healed. The prayer of a righteous person is powerful and effective.
—James 5:16

My mid-life, debilitating health scare was relatively unusual. You will face your own tests and trials that could imperil your ministry. The good news is that you can decide to invest in a prayer life that equips you to weather the challenge, see God at work and keep your ears tuned to His voice.

Letter 2

Administration:

A Recipe for Success

Principle:
Your ability to effectively administer the church's business and operate it for God's glory depends on your ability to grasp the vision God has for your ministry, convert that vision into a manageable strategy and use the strategy to guide your daily decisions and interactions. Losing track of either of the first two elements clouds your decision-making and introduces unnecessary conflict.

Dear Son,

Your transition to senior pastor of Omega Baptist Church first got me thinking about writing this book. As I mentored you in preparation for this critical transition, administration—daily management of the church's affairs in conjunction with associate ministers, deacons, staff and board of trustees—was one of the most-challenging topics to address. These activities consumed most of my Tuesdays through Fridays, and provided some of my most-uplifting moments; as well as the most stressful, disheartening ones. How can you set up yourself for success in this often-perplexing task?

A High-Wire Administrative Challenge

The most-difficult administrative interactions and decisions pivot around questions of vision, strategy and trust. Years after recovery from the lesions on my brain, the fiscal health of our church was strained. Membership numbers had stabilized and we had relocated church operations to the newly-acquired 30-acre property, opening opportunities to expand the impact of our ministry. However, the move came at a cost. While still paying mortgage on the land, we found that the pre-existing buildings were expensive to heat and cool, and required significant infrastructure investments. We might have comfortably weathered these expenses at our peak tithes and offerings, but our numbers were well below what they had been before my health crisis.

A year after we relocated our offices, the church board recommended a series of moves designed to stop the financial bleeding while preserving our ability to incrementally pay off the land and use it selectively for ministry events. Their recommendations included demolition of several of the buildings, including the one we had moved all of our offices. This plan contradicted the vision God had given me for the campus. Deep within, I felt it was critical to have as much activity on the campus as possible. While we still had Sunday worship in our pre-existing sanctuary, we used the campus for Wednesday night Bible study, special events such as baby dedications, staff training and youth activities. I feared that relocating all this activity to the old building would marginalize the new campus and threaten members' commitment to it.

This moment was one of several dramatic cases of tension at the core of effective church administration. As a leader working with business staff members and board trustees who first view the church's challenges from a pragmatic, fact-based perspective, your job is to absorb the realities without always responding as a secular CEO. You have two complicating factors: the spiritual dimensions of the challenge, and the underlying vision God has given you and your church.

Successful church administration is best supported by coordination of the following critical elements:

1. The vision driving your church
2. The strategy deployed to realize the vision
3. Day-to-day administration informed by the vision and strategy

Vision — Bringing Purpose to Life

The *Prayer is Your Fuel Letter* speaks to the many benefits of establishing a moment-by-moment prayer connection with God. Another application of this connection is a clear vision that brings your church's purpose to life in your mind; and ultimately in the minds of your leaders and congregation.

When counseled to relocate church offices and demolish most of the buildings on our new campus — a move that felt like a step backwards — Vanessa and I revisited the purpose God laid on our hearts for Omega Church. Our long-standing mission statement: "We are a people empowered by the Holy Spirit to serve families, communities and the world!" Two elements of our vision included empathetic fellowship focused on meeting spiritual and earthly needs of others, and urban, in-the-streets evangelism geared toward social justice.

This mission and vision had driven acquisition of the new campus, which set a few blocks from our church facility. When the prior owners—who probably knew market demand for the property would not be sky high given Dayton's economic climate—offered it to us, Vanessa and I felt God affirm its fit with the church's purpose. We saw the opportunity to more-concretely affect the surrounding neighborhoods and pour into more lives. While certain risks inherent in acquiring a large campus with aged buildings existed, we weighed the opportunity reflecting on advice from my father in ministry, Reverend M.L. Daniels.

"Rev," he said, "walk through the doors that God opens for you."

For better or worse, I followed that advice and walked through most of the doors God opened to Omega and me. As Reverend Daniels testified, I look back and feel more regret about the few doors I did not walk through than those to which I said, "Yes." Samuel validated this principle:

> *And Samuel said, "Hath the Lord as great delight in burnt offerings and sacrifices, as in obeying the voice of the Lord? Behold, to obey is better than sacrifice, and to hearken than the fat of rams."*
> —1 Samuel 15:22

You cannot reliably evaluate doors that open for your church if you don't have a vision to evaluate them against.

And you cannot develop a vision without taking time to regularly invest in prayer that clarifies God's purpose for your ministry gifts. As your vision forms, be transparent in sharing and socializing it with the leaders of your church. If you don't have a shared vision, how can you effectively pull together and achieve what God has in store for all of you?

I am thankful for the vision, which Omega Church has articulated and nurtured over the years. Our attempts to carry it out and transform our community have not always progressed according to plan or without controversy. However, as I pass the mantle of leadership to you, Joshua, I appreciate God's grace. After fifteen years of sowing into urban ministry and renewal, our church entered a season of harvest. The same campus we vacated to preserve finances is in development. A 26-million-dollar facilities investment will provide local residents with resources for workforce development, education, health care and senior housing. At a time when companies and organizations are exiting our community, Omega's non-profit development corporation is standing with those who might otherwise feel left behind. While insisting on adherence to the strictest standards of quality and ethics, we took the opportunity to include local, minority-owned firms among our vendors and contractors.

God blessed our church with significant ministry success over the years, but I always believed in a vision that moved us toward developments such as these. Our vision went beyond building a big, fancy church and doing revivals; we wanted to serve the community. Without belief in a workable strategy and action plans that help ensure the vision materialized, we probably would not be where we are.

Strategy—Constructing Flexible Plans to Make the Vision Real

Construction of a documented strategic plan is important to help ensure everyone in your church leadership is advancing the core vision and purpose. Several credible books including Rick Warren's *The Purpose Driven Church* and Aubrey Malphurs' *Advanced Strategic Planning*, will help you apply strategic planning principles for the betterment of your church and ministry.

My specific advice regarding strategy is be fluid and dynamic like the Holy Spirit. Document the strategy with an awareness, agreed to with your leadership team, that the details and tactics applied to achieve the underlying goals will never be static. With the passing of time, God will allow challenges and unforeseen opportunities that will refocus your priorities and redirect aspects of your efforts.

We adjusted strategic priorities and tactics multiple times to be in position to live our vision and purpose. Before acquiring the new campus, we embarked on an ambitious partnership with local, state and federal government entities that would have resulted in a new worship center and community center. When the partnership broke down and one entity after another backed out of its commitments to the project, my spirit became troubled. My leadership team and I agreed to withdraw from the partnership. The painful decision disappointed some members and injected tension into our relations with locally powerful people, but history validated my sense that the project was not going to allow Omega to achieve its intended vision and purpose.

As that project ended for us, God assured that He moved me to close one door to pay attention when He opened another. I sensed that the new door would not look much like the prior one. In my experience, prior achievements are not a roadmap to future ones. Stay in communication with God so you have real-time discernment to evaluate each new opportunity.

The president of United Theological Seminary, whom I regularly met with for networking purposes, often inquired about Omega purchasing their campus as they considered relocation. After several inquiries, I prayed and decided to let him state a purchase price.

From a layman's perspective, the stated figure sounded appealing. I discussed the matter with the board. Despite having several professionals with more knowledge about real estate than me, I did not have to sell too many on the idea of the purchase. We agreed that the price was competitive for a starting figure. Our finances were solid, and we had a good record of paying off mortgages in a timely manner.

Thus, the situation that pitted me against the board's recommendation to relocate from the new campus back to original church building. Marginalizing the campus in the eyes of members was of great concern. I wanted as much activity there as possible, so that it stayed prevalent and focused people on helping pay off the mortgage. I feared an out-of-sight-out-of-mind mentality might reduce commitment to eliminate the debt.

I soon realized that I had to emotionally separate from the property. My strong history with the seminary affected my objectivity. I needed the analytical perspective of my board for a balanced, unbiased view. This example is one of many in which listening to God started with listening to the people He placed on my leadership team.

God gave me a peace that I had to listen to all of my board members, including the few who regularly got on my nerves! The Board doesn't always agree with Vanessa or me, but in the cases where they told us "no", they often got it right.

So, even though my heart cried within me, I saw the wisdom of their counsel. As we returned offices and core operations to the original building, I accepted God's assurance that we would move back to the campus. We again took a strategic detour on our march toward a vision in which our leadership firmly believed. Moving off campus was painful, but doing what made sense was clearly in God's will.

Strategic adjustments don't have to be reactive. After we moved and demolished many of the new campus buildings, I was blessed with reflection time at a Harvard University Executive Leadership study program. I was inspired to author a document envisioning ways Omega's community development corporation—which had a robust reputation for investing in the welfare of at-risk children and other underprivileged populations—could spearhead development of the campus. I realized we had been too focused on establishing a new worship center and core operations on the campus, when we had functional space at our existing property. Concentrating on campus development to provide services that improve people's lives put us on a successful path.

While our progress reminds me of what can be accomplished when you focus on a goal, walking the campus reminds me that you are never really done with strategic plans. When you remove one barrier, you expose a mountain range that was blocked by the obstacle you just cleared! The work never stops and there is always more to do. That's more reason to pause, rest and acknowledge God's provision as you achieve each milestone victory.

Day-to-Day Administration

So you have your vision, and built the perfect, yet flexible, ten-point strategic plan. Now it is time for the "ivory tower" nature of vision and strategy to collide with the daily reality of administering your church. To master this challenge, surround yourself with the right people.

Some churches and non-profit organizations are unfairly accused of hiring incompetent or unqualified employees. Maybe that is why I initially made some wrong decisions regarding staffing and leadership. I hired people and selected church leaders based almost entirely on professional skills, especially those I did not have. That was a good start, but I soon learned that I did not account for compatibility. As you go through the thorny process of managing the church vision and seeking God's guidance on how to alter strategic plans, you want to work with people whom you enjoy spending time. Choose people with whom you can disagree in a professional, collaborative manner. We don't "agree to disagree" and go our separate ways; we productively discuss our differences until we arrive at an agreed decision.

I was inspired with distinct standards to select my team after reading a November 2003 article in *Premier Christianity*. The author, Pastor Bill Hybels of Willow Creek Community Church, wrote about the "Three Cs" when hiring staff:

- Character. Select those who have a record of being truth-tellers, covenant-keepers and being more

focused on crediting others for team accomplishments than seeking their own glory.
- Competence. Be clear about the minimum professional standards needed for them to succeed. Start by focusing on those who most-clearly exceed them. Those top candidates still have to pass the potentially toughest test: the chemistry screen.
- Chemistry. Do they mesh well with the rest of the staff? Do you like them and find you want to spend time with them? If not, clearing the first two criteria may not matter.

While applying these screens, keep another of Hybels' tips in mind regarding staffing: Don't overlook your congregation. Whether paid staff roles or seats on the church board, seek among your congregation for members with gifts that could make them competitive candidates.

Once your team is in place, it is time to deal with the reality of conflict. Conflict resolution may be one of the least appreciated of the unique challenges that confront spiritual leaders. If you lead a church with more than a few dozen members, at any given time, ministry leaders, business managers, security and custodial staff make hundreds of decisions. Guess who gets to serve as the public face whenever any of those decisions leaves someone dissatisfied.

Employ the following practices to most-effectively manage conflict:

1. When you and a member of your staff or leadership team need to have a difficult conversation, address it one-on-one as soon as possible. As long as you are in control of your emotions and manage your

words, you can say almost anything to a person in such a context.

2. If you have to negotiate a conflict between two people and know which one is "wrong," in need of correction or will have to be overruled, handle that person with the same respect you show to the other one. You never want to embarrass anyone.

3. Encourage free, but orderly, expression of dissenting thoughts and comments in staff meetings. As long as they remain respectful toward you and others, you want all staff to feel free to speak their minds. It is best that that they share what is on their heart because you cannot address unexpressed issues.

4. While God spoke to Elijah in a "still, small voice," He is not limited to one mode of communication. Sometimes, He speaks through messengers we would not choose. Be open to receive.

If you're like me, you have that pesky board officer whose seeming sole purpose is to second guess what you believe God revealed to you. Nine times out of ten, that officer is not alone! Keep your ears open when they speak because unless they clearly have a personal agenda, others in the congregation feel the same way. You can often get advance warnings about course corrections from these officers, even if you file them under the adage: keep your friends close and your enemies closer.

If they become a true enemy, that changes the equation. Exercise your authority with great care. Unless the individual does something unethical or immoral, maneuvering to get them off the board can backfire if not done with great forethought and humility. If you handle people harshly, even your greatest ally will question whether they can provide you with candid advice. And for people who have passed the character, competence and chemistry screens, you want their feedback and news, even when it is not good. If you are going to learn from each experience and ensure that projects, events and activities generate the intended results, you have to be thick-skinned. Take in negative feedback and prescriptive suggestions.

Growing up in ministry, I had the opportunity to hear pastors in conversation with their board members and staff. I learned how they managed conflict, but I also learned the perils of autocratic leadership. Hollering and screaming is counter-productive. Be an approachable leader who is genuinely interested in the thoughts and counsel of your team.

Don't feel obligated to say something just because you are in charge. I worked with seminary leaders and pastors whose constant attempts to appear intellectual by filling the air with empty talk reflected poorly on them. Their example taught me to be quiet when I have nothing to add. In church meetings and community board meetings, when I speak it counts. That may be why I am invited to serve on boards, locally and beyond.

Considering the many ways in which your leadership team—especially unpaid staff, associate ministers, deacons and trustees who moonlight to support the church—goes beyond the call of duty to support you, show your appreciation. Take care of those who take care of you, your family and your church. When these individuals face challenges and difficulties—illness, bereavement, job loss—I don't let an associate minister comfort or pray with them. I perform such functions to express my gratitude for their efforts. It is the least I can do.

Tips to Chair Board and Staff Meetings

1. Open and close every meeting with prayer. Use your God-given power as your calling card to initiate important interactions.
2. Newell Wert, a veteran dean at United Theological Seminary, taught me when to conclude a meeting. "Wait for someone to say the main point with which you agree, then wrap it up!"
3. Conduct battles that require confronting groups of staff or trustees at the time and place of your choosing. Do the necessary homework to get your ducks in a row, speak with the appropriate people and formulate your argument before you engage with your opponent(s). Don't shrink from asserting your right to decide when the matter will be discussed and a "winner" determined.
4. Take your time! Regardless of the issue or the conflict, it is impossible to take back something wrongly said or ill-timed. If you need more time to address an issue, take it.

Administration—An Adventurous Necessity

As pastor, you will spend more time performing "soft" tasks like administration and networking than the splashy, high-profile activities of preaching and speaking before large audiences. Embrace the adventure inherent in administration, instead of shying from it. Take time to grasp the vision that will drive your church and pursue its realization with flexible strategic action plans. Watch God work as you select a "Three Cs" leadership team, manage conflict and build team loyalty by showing your leaders appreciation for their dedication and sacrifice. You will accelerate your church's fulfillment of its God-given purpose.

Letter 3

Worship!

Principle:

God is spirit, and His worshipers must worship in the Spirit and in truth.
—John 4:24 NIV

This simple statement gets at the root of the lessons I learned about providing a fulfilling worship experience. To worship in Spirit and in truth, set the example for your worship leaders. Use empathy to provide a well-managed service that meets the needs of your core congregation while staying true to the style of worship God planted in you and your worship team.

Dear Son,

My recommendations for delivering a worship experience break down into three primary areas:

1. **Trust God to help you hear the voice of your customer.** Keep your eyes and ears open to monitor

the extent to which each element of worship is meeting your parishioners' needs.

2. **Be an authentic worship leader.** From the sermon to the nature of the praise and worship, don't chase popularity mimicking a preaching style or the booming mega-church. Trust God to use the gifts He has provided you and your worship leaders.

3. **Apply spiritual and administrative leadership.** Your job is not finished once you hire that charismatic minister of music or update the order of service. Pay attention to building maintenance, audio/video equipment and other factors that can enhance — or diminish — the worship experience.

Managing the Worship Experience

Don't be tempted into thinking that your primary obligation regarding worship is delivery of the sermon. As senior pastor, you are called to exercise your anointing and influence over the entire worship experience.

On a regular basis, consider service from the perspective of a first-time visitor. From the moment they pull into the church parking lot until they return to their car, what is their experience? When do they first encounter a church member or employee? Does that person smile and interact with them in a welcoming way? What impressions does the exterior of the church and its condition leave on visitors? When they first step into the main lobby, are they greeted and ushered into the sanctuary? What thoughts or emotions might they experience as they enter the sanctuary?

These people trust you with a couple hours of their lives. Why do you think they are going out of their way to do that? Are you offering a worship service that respects their time and makes it a worthwhile investment? Have they come to hear announcements of upcoming events, or to be fussed at about an event they missed? No, they came to worship God! Give them what they came for and they will come back. Church officials who want to keep announcements and other business front and center will probably challenge you, but prioritizing the needs of worshippers comes first.

Ponder these questions from the perspective of a member who lives this experience every week. Are you providing an environment that sets up each parishioner for a fruitful worship experience? Weigh these questions regularly, and compare findings with your leadership team. The answers should direct your decisions about the worship service, building, grounds and ways in which ushers, greeters and church leaders interact with visitors and faithful members.

The first step toward a fulfilling worship experience is a congregation that shows genuine care for each person entering the building.

Pastors tend to put so much pressure on winning new members with the sermon that other transformative details are overlooked. As a young preacher in training, I visited numerous churches with the intention of choosing a home church that could look out for my family while I traveled on business. Too often, we encountered churches where we were shooed out of unmarked reserved seats. At times, we were treated—or ignored—in ways that drove us away faster than any imperfect sermon could. Intentional, thoughtful management of your church's worship experience provides your congregation with spiritual care and feeding while fostering the membership growth that every church needs to prosper.

Scripture Motivation: Why We Worship

As you consider how to manage the worship experience, I point you toward scriptural citations that can help direct these important decisions. They remind me of the types of emotions flooding members and visitors seeking a relevant worship experience. The most-common categories of worship needs include pain and loss, celebrations and growth in God. Your challenge is to strike a balance in any worship experience so worshippers at every point on the spectrum are addressed.

- Worshipping in the Face of Pain and Loss
  King David demonstrated what it means to worship in the face of loss and pain. His baby (the product of his adultery with Bathsheba) died. He prayed and prayed, but the baby was not spared. I cannot imagine the pain that comes from the loss of a child, and the guilt spurred by knowledge that your actions may have been part of the cause. As one who saw both parents die relatively young, the loss of loved ones can feel too great to bear. But look at what David did after the baby died:

  Then David got up from the ground. After he had washed, put on lotions and changed his clothes, he went into the house of the Lord and worshipped.
  —2 Samuel 12:20 NIV

  Taking our grief seriously, and bringing it into the worship service, is the first step toward lasting recovery. As the orchestrator of the worship service, always incorporate elements that will help grieving worshippers take that first step.

- Worshipping to Celebrate Who God is and What He's Done

    Shout for joy to the Lord, all the Earth. Worship the Lord with gladness; come before Him with joyful songs. Know that the Lord is God. It is He who made us, and we are His; we are His people, the sheep of His pasture. Enter His gates with thanksgiving and His courts with praise; give thanks to Him and praise His name. For the Lord is good and His love endures forever; His faithfulness continues through all generations.
    —Psalm 100:1-5 NIV

The infectious joy that bursts from this passage evokes the motivation driving many worshippers entering your service. Whether experiencing "good times" or blessed with a spiritual perspective that overrides challenging circumstances, the ability to celebrate God frees us to concentrate closely on His pure, blameless nature. When worshippers get lost in the goodness of God, the devil has a hard time finding them. The worship service should consistently provide opportunities to celebrate God's presence.

- Worshipping to Grow in God

    So that Christ may dwell in your hearts through faith. And I pray that you, being rooted and

> *established in love, may have power, together with all the Lord's holy people, to grasp how wide and long and high and deep is the love of Christ, and to know this love that surpasses knowledge — that you may be filled to the measure of all the fullness of God.*
> —Ephesians 3:17-19 NIV

When you consider this all-powerful, all-knowing God who is the core creator of universes known and unknown, it is a wonder that we could aspire to an intimate relationship with Him. The sermon and the entire worship experience should point worshippers toward a pathway to this increasingly intimate, insightful walk with God.

How often have you heard former members of a church say, "I left because I wasn't being fed"? The best way to protect your church from such charges is to center everything on God's Word. Feed the people His Word in a way that makes its teachings — and the God behind them — more accessible. Some members will still leave, but you can rest assured that you provided a nourishing worship experience.

Listen for the Voice of Your Consumer

Although the demands of pastoring are distinctly different from those of a corporate executive, the positions offer mutual learning opportunities. Years ago, Gardner Taylor, known as the "dean of preachers," paraphrased a story attributed to economist and business professor, Russ Roberts. Professor Roberts posted this popular story on CafeHayek.com in January 2010.

Roberts told of a pet food company that created a new dog food product and rolled out a massive marketing campaign to introduce it. When initial sales were disappointing, the company fired its first-rate advertising agency and started over with a new agency and campaign. Sales again came in below expectations, in fact, worse than the initial campaign.

The desperate CEO called the entire leadership team for a brainstorming session. The group analyzed both campaigns in hopes of crafting a third, successful campaign. The executives applied sophisticated statistical analyses in their search for an answer. One vice president believed that the mix of television and print ads was poorly executed. Another argued that the previous campaigns had been too subtle and failed to prominently spotlight the product's greatest features. Still another argued that the TV ad campaign focused too much on spots during sporting events, and not enough on regular programming with a broader demographic. He was contradicted by a peer who believed the campaigns should have invested more in sports programming ads.

After hours of debate, the CEO felt little had been accomplished. He asked for additional theories to explain the failed launches. A newly-hired executive raised her hand. When recognized, she said, "Maybe," with the hesitation of a junior employee, "the dogs don't like it."

Sometimes the answer is right in front of us. The life application of this story is not that church leaders shouldn't make wise use of the latest management tools to structure and administer the worship service. The lesson: the church must focus on what matters most when structuring worship, and not get caught up in distractions. God selected you to pastor this church and every church is different. While we may learn from what other churches do, it doesn't mean that your church parishioners need or want it.

Compared with those bumbling pet food executives, you have an advantage: direct, frequent access to your consumer. Your congregation is the "target market" for the worship service, and you get to interact with them regularly. Invest in building connections that allow you to refine worship to address shared needs (more on this topic later). Start by ensuring you and your leadership team foster informal, frank communication in which members provide feedback about recent worship experiences. If you hear the same comments from multiple people, take note.

What If I Build a Worship Service and No One Comes? Trust in Your Target Market

In some contexts, evolving your worship service in response to the voice of your consumer is challenging. If God called you to preside over aggressive growth at your church, or if membership is declining at a rate that endangers the survival of the institution, you will feel compelled to cater to the murky needs and expectations of people who are not seated among the congregation.

I have experienced many types of membership growth challenges: amazing organic growth in the early years of ministry when we didn't have a consistent worship facility, intentionally managed spikes as we matured into a well-established body of worship and declines associated with local and personal developments. Omega was a "hot church" for many years, experiencing unexplained growth patterns and others that traced to programming and worship updates, which the Lord inspired. However, the combination of my illness and Dayton's economic and population declines reduced our congregation by hundreds.

For all of its challenges, our "wilderness experience" provided clarity about the type of parishioner to which our calling and worship style was best suited. Years of popularity with people from every lifestyle flowing through our doors had blurred the focus on our core membership. As the crowd thinned, we discerned the profile of those who remained: people who were intentional about using each worship service to chew on Scripture, learn more about God and apply lessons in their daily lives. While we always worked to structure a worship service that was inclusive, when this profile emerged, we steered our worship toward honoring these people's needs.

Experience taught me that when you make your worship service an authentic representation of you and your leadership team's worship, you will find your intended target market of worshippers. Remember that attendance and membership trends may be volatile, and the nature of your core membership may evolve. At challenging times, God is changing the congregation or transforming you as its shepherd. When you keep that in mind, you can focus on being true to your calling, while remaining open to God's voice when it is time for course correction. Sometimes, He calls you to "be still" in the face of declining membership, at others you may be led to implement radical changes. Keeping close to God and staying familiar with His voice is the only way to know where He is moving.

You are God's instrument. Follow His leadership and you won't have to worry if people will follow. As God worked on me, Omega had five different pastors. Each version of me honored God. God is not honored in plenty of churches, and Christ is not exalted. Don't you trust God to send the right people to your church if you are doing His will?

Timeless Worship Management Principles

As you tend to the ever-present challenges of matching worship to the needs of your congregation, keep some general management principles in mind. These principles are less spiritual and more administrative in nature; however, that is just as important.

1. A flowing, interconnected service makes people comfortable and helps open their hearts.

    Omega operates with no silent periods during service unless it is called for as part of the sermon. Some churches allow for plenty of silence. All goes quiet as the congregation awaits the next song, speaker or presentation. Worshippers responded more positively to an environment that established a consistent rhythm and atmosphere to facilitate their connection to God. We instructed our ministers of music to keep the flow of service fluid. Any transition in service was accompanied by background music that built on the emotions stirred by the previous song, speaker or presentation.

    A similar motivation affected our decision to minimize the impromptu sharing of individual congregants' testimonies. Every so often, the Spirit moves me to open a call for these; however, due to unpredictable length and potentially questionable theology, testimonies are likely to disrupt parishioners' worship experience. The church can foster sharing of testimonials through Sunday school and small group Bible studies.

2. Seek new opportunities to get a broader cross-section of the congregation involved in worship.

   Early in the life of Omega Church, the Lord revealed that if our worship experience was to benefit everyone in the congregation, we needed to have diverse worship leaders. This started with traditional activities like Youth Sundays, a senior choir and a men's chorus. It expanded to less-common developments including liturgical dance, mime, youth and teen spoken word and gospel rap. We sought new ways to offer a relevant worship opportunity, which eased their ability to relate scriptural lessons to daily living.

3. Pastoring and preaching are not the same thing.

   My father in ministry, Rev. Daniels, lived this out for me. In the three years I studied under him, he did not preach. He riled up the congregation at various points of each service, but he never delivered the formal sermon. All the while, he was very much the pastor. When my son, Joshua, preaches, people stop me in the vestibule to compliment the entire worship service. Now that my senior pastor role is part-time, I am still responsible for the character and quality of the worship experience. Preaching is a part of pastoring, but in the context of managing the worship experience, it is one of many elements to oversee.

4. Don't spiritualize away the necessary physical logistics affecting worship.

   Worship logistics are rarely fun or glamorous, but attention to detail protects your parishioners' worship experience. Does your church have the right equipment to support an effective worship service? Don't waste money or lose focus, but obtain and use the best equipment God has blessed you to afford.

   Dr. Leonard Sweet, former president of United Theological Seminary, often advocated for the role of technology in Christian ministry. When people told him that technology was demonic, he responded that skeptics once said the same about the printing press. Considering the many ways the church's expansion was aided by the invention of Gutenberg's printing press, technology is nothing to be feared or disdained. Whether assessing technology that supports the worship experience for live attendees or "streamers" who view it online, approach it with confidence that the big God we serve can help us use it for His glory.

   Granted, some churches pay too much attention to their audio-video equipment. They have state-of-the-art technology, but the content lacks substance and does not connect with worshippers' deepest needs. The challenge is to strike an optimal balance. Functional, effective equipment raises the quality of the worship experience. While dead microphones, deafening speakers or unreliable screens will obstruct the message God has for your congregation and may cause headaches.

Sound and visual quality are affected by the infrastructure of the church. To the extent possible, don't let audio, visual, or HVAC-related issues sabotage an empowering worship experience. Refer to the letter on administration (page 35) to ensure you hire qualified people to oversee infrastructure and audio-video production.

Be True to God's Call

The two most-important pillars of worship strategy are authenticity and planning. The core of worship is honoring God-given gifts—yours and your worship team; while maintaining vigilance over the ongoing administration of the worship experience. When responsible stewardship eliminates obstacles that could disrupt the movement of the Holy Spirit, you set up your worshippers for a supernatural encounter.

Daryl Ward

Letter 4

Preparing Your Sermon

Principle:
Patience is the most-important quality to bring to your sermon preparation. Patience is required to sit with your Scripture text, study academically, pray fervently, draw on the knowledge and experiences of others to interpret it, and mine your life experiences to bring its messages to life. When you commit to this work, your reward will be a narrative that resounds far beyond applause and hallelujahs.

Dear Son,

This letter is a mini-workshop. I drew from the course outline I prepared for a hermeneutics course I teach. Merriam-Webster defines hermeneutics as "the study of the methodological principles of interpretation (as of the Bible)."

First Things First

Each time you step into a pulpit, your job is to properly interpret the Word of God. Keeping that purpose clear in my mind brings me great peace. I don't get it right every time, but I know the road that will get listeners to the right answer. Seeing and following that road requires loving and studying the Scriptures.

Before you prepare any sermon, remind yourself that when He called you, He intended for you to be a walking embodiment of His teachings. You don't just preach with your mouth. Your movements, gestures and voice inflections should communicate consistently with your messages. This call is not to perfection, but understand that you may have to preach your best sermons on the bus or a street corner. Your most-effective message may be a bag of groceries delivered to the victims of a house fire, not an eruditely worded sermon delivered to a mega church. Embracing this reality will enrich your preparatory process.

Step 1: How Do I Select the Underlying Scripture?

You may not realize the extent to which preachers struggle to choose source material for sermons. When I attended my first National Baptist Preachers Conventions, I was stunned to hear exhibit hall vendors calling out, "Get your Mother's Day and Thanksgiving sermons here!" It does not take long to sympathize with those so desperate that such hucksters are encouraged to sell their wares.

Even for those of us who have no problem developing sermon material, many contemporary Baptist preachers take cues from the contemporary culture. In an age where the church faces a unique struggle to prove its relevance to millennial and younger audiences, wise preachers must acknowledge and speak to the realities of today's culture. Consider, however, this cautionary question: Who is in charge, the culture or Christ? Preaching that focuses almost exclusively on contemporary realities can make you popular, but it won't necessarily make you prophetic.

Every preacher should follow the Holy Spirit when preparing sermons. Events occurring in your personal life, community or nationally may inspire you to focus on a specific scriptural passage and set of life applications. I have experienced that type of inspiration many times, but for consistency, consult *The Common Lectionary*. This book is a collection of Scriptures matched to days on which they can be applied for Protestant worship services. If consulted on a consistent, weekly basis, *The Lectionary* will take you through the entire canon of Scripture in three years.

Making myself the sole arbiter of my scriptural focus can be limiting. I could study and preach about a favorite book like Luke for two years, if I followed my heart. Using *The Lectionary* motivates me to preach the whole counsel of God, and not get tangled in the same few Old Testament books, Gospels or Revelation. Whether contemporary events or specific life application messages God placed in me, I can usually find a passage from *The Lectionary* that is in tune with them. The idea that *The Lectionary* could be relevant was ludicrous to me, until I was forced to use it in seminary. So don't "knock it before you try it."

You are not tied to *The Lectionary*. Some weeks may require you to freelance, while others have specific preaching topics. You may be led to conduct series focused on a particular book of the Bible. I find great peace in knowing that outside of these "one-off" weeks or series, I have a carefully selected set of passages from which to seek inspiration. *The Lectionary* also keeps me in tune with the church calendar and critical events such as Advent and Lent.

This broadens my perspective and sense of unity with fellow church leaders and worshippers.

Step 2: Stay with the Text

Once you have made your scriptural selection, read and re-read the passage. Don't be too quick to start consulting commentaries; take the time to sit with the text. Read it in multiple translations including King James, New King James, English Standard Version, New Revised Standard Version, The Message, New Living and Good News.

As much as possible, stay with the text. Don't add a bunch of texts and race through the Old and New Testaments. Meditate on the text so it can teach you. The old preachers said, "Whatever you need, it is in there. Keep looking…and pray!"

Come to the Scripture with an open mind for limitless interpretation or life application of the passage. Be open to wherever the passage takes you. As you read and re-read, ask yourself the following questions and journal the answers:

1. What questions does the passage raise in your mind? Consider the context in which the events occurred or the messages preached. It could relate to historical disagreements about the passage's interpretation.
2. What words in the passage—any translation of it—jump out at you? Why?
3. What other Scriptures come to mind as you study this one? Why?
4. What stories from your life, or the experience of those you know, would help illustrate points raised by the passage?

Step 3: Exegesis — Interpreting Your Text

The online version of Collins Dictionary defines exegesis as "an explanation and interpretation of a piece of writing after very careful study." Effective interpretation of your text starts with ongoing dependence on tools like online concordances. I rely on *Strong's Concordance* for citations of specific words in the passage. This practice leads to a greater understanding of those words, their intended meanings and finding corroborating scriptural passages that further clarify the message.

Use concordances and related tools to seek historical contexts, and grasp what people of that day meant when they spoke the words enshrined in Scripture. During your preparation, devote time studying words, even if you have not studied Greek or Hebrew. A concordance can guide you to the origin of words; identify Greek or Hebrew meanings and common translations.

The root meanings of many words differ significantly from the corresponding English translation assigned to them. To preach intelligently about your passage, be mindful of such distinctions. Consider the myriad meanings of "love" in Greek:

- Agapé is unconditional love as in John 3:16;
- Eros is romantic attraction as in 2 Timothy 3:2 and
- Phileo is brotherly love as in John 5:20

Most Christians are aware of these definitions of love; however, many words have multiple meanings depending on the context. You are called to invest the time required to rightly divide the intended meaning of the words in any passage addressed in your sermon.

Step 4: Consult Commentaries

Now that you invested time and effort to become intimately familiar with your text, you are ready to seek insight from one or more reliable commentaries. A wealth of options are available including Blue Note Bible, an online source, and Logos Software, a powerful search engine designed to support Bible study. Logos is expensive, but when it comes to sermon preparation materials, the investment is worth it.

As you gather perspectives from commentary and similar sources, be open to new ideas about how to bring your text's interpretation to life. Keep a notepad (a physical one or phone app) on your nightstand to capture inspirations that hit overnight or during times of rest. Use online sources like those cited above to test your ideas against related books and other published sermon material.

While I urge preachers to make their sermons unique to avoid copycat messages, you may find inspiration from others when seeking ways to illustrate the lessons in your text. Draw from your life experiences to drive home a point, using examples from others to complement or reinforce, if necessary. Whatever you use to solidify your message, make sure it aligns with the text.

Finally, when reviewing commentaries and other informative sources, ensure you study the full context of your text. Account for Scriptures that precede and follow it. What additional light does that shed? Understand the era in which each passage was written, the cultural context that influenced it, decisions and words of everyone depicted. You will find something that makes your message more insightful.

Step 5: Integrate

At this point, you have a wealth of material at your fingertips. It is time to bring together the fruits of your research to form a clear narrative. Your most-important ingredients will be:

1. Your original ideas. This fruit includes the initial interpretations and messages the Spirit shares with you. Capture ways the text is relevant to contemporary issues and realities affecting your worshippers' daily lives here, too.
2. Your life experiences. Incorporate your relevant experiences to reveal vulnerability and connection with the audience.
3. Exegete material. Your study of the translated and original meanings of the text will result in a body of material that improves your ability to interpret the Scriptures.
4. Materials referenced from commentaries and others' sermons. While you won't use this content verbatim, inspiration can be drawn by analyzing their understanding of the main text and surrounding passages.

Pull together this valuable material to form a rough draft of the narrative that will drive your sermon. This initial version will contain material that will not make the final cut. For now, incorporate every piece of information that plausibly supports a coherent message that ultimately answers "So what?" about the text.

Step 6: Edit, Edit, Edit
This critical step is not easy. Above all else, be merciless. The only way to respect the flow of service and your congregants' time, is to eliminate material unearthed during the preparatory process. Ask God for discernment to know what stays and what goes. If you feel a slight bit uneasy about an illustration, experience or idea, exclude it from the outline; however, save it for future use.

Step 7: Build an Outline that Flows with the Scripture Passage
A seminary professor told me that it is okay to preach your sermon points in any order. I prefer preaching at about a seventh-grade level. Jason Kottke, a highly-accomplished web designer and blogger, titled one of his blogs, *If You Can't Explain Something in Simple Terms, You Don't Understand It* (June 15, 2017). That logic applies to sermons.

You can't preach what you don't understand, and much of your audience won't understand, if you don't communicate in simple terms. Don't preach to impress. Preach to convert, inspire and educate. Reverend Daniels advised me to never draft a sermon attempting to draw shouts or applause.

Keep it simple. Order your outline so key points flow with the scriptural text. This technique allows the audience to follow your narrative and avoids those unfortunate moments where they whisper to the person next to them, "Where is he going with this?"

Step 8: Your Final Product
Pastor H. Beecher Hicks, Sr., under whom I accepted my call to ministry, invited me to Washington, D.C. to preach at

Metropolitan Baptist Church. Preaching that Sunday turned out to be intimidating for two reasons. Metropolitan was among the largest, most-politically connected African-American churches in the District. The nation—and, in particular, D.C.—suffered the tragedies of September 11, 2001 a few days before my arrival.

I was bewildered. Why had God chosen me, a pastor from a mid-sized Ohio city, to address these "Black elite" of the nation's Capital at such a horrific time? The importance of the moment was not lost on me. I prayed often as I prepared my message.

Despite the painstaking nature of sermon preparation, minutes into its delivery, it was clear that this hour would not be my finest. Whether my message, delivery or both, I did an awful job connecting with the congregation. I didn't have to mine receiving-line comments to discern whether the sermon was a success. From the pulpit, I observed nonverbal cues that communicated the congregation had tuned me out.

Pastor Hicks' subsequent counsel crystallized what my sermon lacked. "In any situation or circumstance, Daryl, it is our job as preachers to speak *hope!*"

I lost clarity due to distractions that often accompany preaching away from one's home church. Caught up in the pressures of speaking to a large, distinguished audience at a unique moment in history, I invested academically and intellectually into sermon preparation—analyzing, exegeting and prophesying. That was a fine place to start, but I forgot to simplify the message and speak to the most-immediate needs of my audience. I violated the wise counsel of Reverend Daniels, who had long ago suggested that I not let the sophistication of my audience complicate my message. "Take a grain of sand and point out the majesty of God."

Your final sermon results from the combination of the mysteries of God's grace, world events, your life experience and your gift. As you review the final draft and prepare to practice its delivery, avoid my fate at Metropolitan. Ensure you return to that central "So what?" question.

If I could have back my preparatory period for that sermon, I would answer that question first. I'm confident that I would have realized the audience needed a message of hope. Don't fast forward through the steps and never finalize your sermon without chewing and digesting the "So what?" question. If the answer doesn't leap to mind, neither you — nor your sermon — is ready.

Letter 5

Preaching

Principle:
Whether preparing a sermon, delivering it or collecting feedback, three principles should power your efforts. Go the extra mile to ensure that you deliver messages that glorify God *and* respect the time invested by parishioners. In every aspect of your persona as a preacher, embrace your authentic gifts and experiences. Remember: God called *you* to preach. Don't let competing opportunities distract you from using your preaching gifts to serve your congregation above all others.

Dear Son,
Too often, aspiring ministers confuse the call to preach with the call to pastor, but they are not the same. Pastoring encompasses the full scope of topics addressed in these letters, whereas preaching is only one of a pastor's critical duties.

I discussed concerns about pastoral candidates with weak administrative or leadership skills with Reverend M.L. Daniels. I worried that newly-hired pastors who wowed a big church with recycled "hit" sermons would be in over their heads and set up for failure.

Reverend Daniels didn't seem concerned. "Don't worry about the size of the church. The new pastor will get it down to the size he can handle!"

The sermons you deliver can have a tangible effect on your church's journey toward its God-given mission. Not only is preaching often the most-memorable element of worship, alongside praise and worship it will determine whether visitors turn into members. The extent to which those receiving the right hand of fellowship become long-term members who tithe, serve and perhaps lead alongside you is a direct result of preaching.

Preparing Your Sermon

My years in ministry—as a preacher and observer of leading preachers—have revealed sermon preparation best practices every pastor should consider.

1. A key checkpoint: "So What?"

    As noted in the *Preparing Your Sermon Letter* (page 63), no matter how brilliantly it seems everything is coming together, set aside time to ask this potentially inconvenient question. Review the exercise at the beginning of the *Worship Letter* (page 49) to put yourself in their shoes. Will the current message give the listener a clear answer to "So what?"

    Your job is to educate the worshipper about the Scripture, what it says about the people and circumstances involved, and most-importantly how it applies to their daily lives. Make sure you are hearing from the Holy Spirit about the scriptural interpretation and application. Clear interpretations can spur healthy movement and life change. Connect the dots between your research and what the audience needs. Does a world-weary visitor need to hear the exegetical detail that inspired your suggested life applications? The answer sounds obvious, but avoiding this trap requires your close attention.

Vet your message through the lens of whether it can make a difference in the listeners' lives. To make sure each point is user-friendly, ask yourself if you could answer a parishioner who asked, "Why are you telling me this, Pastor?"

2. Don't get carried away with quotes. Trust your voice.

   Punctuating a key thought or observation with witty, wise or amusing quotes from others is tempting. Celebrities, comedians, politicians and pastors are popular sources for this type of material. You can often find a place for illuminating or humorous quotes from others; however, use them in moderation. Each time you use someone else's words, you step aside and allow God to speak through that individual, not you.

   Avoid the first easy cliché or refrain that pops into your head. God has called you to preach, and intends to move through *your* words. With the exception of a point that can be illuminated by a third-party quote, take time in sermon preparation to "bring it home" in your words and life experience. God wants you to think and be as unique as possible in your expression.

Sharing your "day in the life" personal stories will be relatable and relevant to your parishioners.

3. Bless your audience with genuine, measured transparency.

   Part of relying on your own words and experiences is a transparent spirit. You want to be transparent so your audience can look through you to see God. The first step to transparency is a commitment to living a godly life, so you have no shame about what people see in you. You do not have to be perfect or have the Christian walk mastered, but you must present a soul that is "pressing toward the mark."

   At a doctoral intensive I attended with prominent ministers, the late Dr. Samuel Dewitt Proctor said, "You have deacons and trustees who are working long hours on their jobs [while] supporting your ministry. They tithe so you have time to read, reflect and write. How do some of us repay them? By sleeping with their wives, getting drunk and wasting time playing video games. We must study to show ourselves approved!" Print his urgent call to action on your heart in all caps.

   When you share your story in an authentic, transparent manner, you give the audience a piece of yourself and build a bond that can foster long-term pastor-parishioner relationships.

   Be strategic about the extent to which you work your testimony into the message. You can't be the subject of every sermon. Leonard Sweet, a mentor, introduced me to the importance of transparency while cautioning to apply it with care. He said, "I don't want to cannibalize myself."

Once you share a revealing or dramatic story from your life, you can't retract it. For years following my illness, I referenced my suffering and healing journey because of its life-altering influence. As time passed, I needed to reference other ways God worked in my life.

4. The value of a good manuscript.

Early in my career, I witnessed the habits of Charles Booth, a pastor with an incredible mind and gift of preaching. As service began, Dr. Booth sat with a printed manuscript of his sermon text. Throughout the worship service, he scanned the manuscript, reading and re-reading it. When he entered the pulpit to preach, he left the script in his chair and masterfully delivered the message as if it had just occurred to him.

Writing my sermon and then reading it multiple times works for me as well. Having important thoughts on the page allows me to test the material and chew on whether it will connect, is clear, relatable and doctrinally sound. Although I try not to rely heavily on the manuscript once I step to the podium, I find it a valuable developmental tool that I can reference during delivery, as needed.

Whether you choose to operate as a "manuscript preacher," I suggest opening each sermon by accepting intervention of the Holy Spirit. With the benefit of your manuscript, you have a reliable blueprint, but always let the Lord build on your work and use you in those critical moments.

5. Set a sermon length that respects people's time.

   This principle was noted as a core element of managing the worship service (page 49), but some weary churchgoers would say it's more urgent when it comes to sermon delivery! Avoid a "runaway" sermon by targeting a specific run time. I shoot for 20 minutes. Since I was taught to spend one hour in study for every minute in the pulpit, I invest at least 20 hours of preparation every week.

   Preacher-pastors should not "riff" and run off at the mouth. Another value of preparing a detailed sermon manuscript is that it helps critically evaluate main points, transitions and every element of the message. This audience granted me a maximum of two hours of their time. If we run over the implicitly agreed duration of service, they may feel disrespected and not bother returning. Therefore, the length of my sermon needs to fit within that timeframe accounting for praise and worship, offering and any special activities that week.

   Use preparation time to evaluate each scriptural exposition, story and explanation against the question, "Is this absolutely necessary?" Be a good steward of the precious time that people have entrusted to you.

   At Omega, we restricted sermon run time while moving it higher in the order of service; before offering and announcements. The intent is to spotlight the Word while attendees have more energy and focus. Ordering service in this way aligns the needs of members and visitors. The strategy only pays off for parishioners and the church if you are efficient and wise with your sermon's run time.

A Point about Delivery

A few years after seminary training, my ability to take constructive criticism was tested. I invited Leonard Sweet, president of the seminary at which I worked, to an event I moderated at Tabernacle Baptist Church, where I served as associate minister. At the conclusion of the event, Leonard, who had already been a great help to my development as a seminarian and aspiring pastor, stunned me with his reaction to my moderator skills.

Leonard, who is not African-American, struck me as embarrassed and amused as he gave it to me straight.

He said, "Listening to you, I kept wondering, 'who is that old Black man from Mississippi speaking up there?' That's not you, Daryl. You are a highly educated young man full of charisma and humor. I heard none of that from you."

It took a while to push past a sense of anger at Leonard's remarks, but I am thankful for how his counsel helped me. He recommended that I read an article about how preachers can find their authentic voice by Thomas H. Troeger. While I initially felt ridiculed, I saw that Leonard was challenging me to honor the uniqueness God created in me, and develop an authentic public speaking/preaching style.

I encourage you to avoid mimicking the styles of others. Instead, gain relevant insight from Dr. Samuel Dewitt Proctor's timeless publications including *The Substance of Things Hoped For*, *The Certain Sound of the Trumpet* and *How*

Shall They Hear? Make books like these part of your ongoing spiritual journey. Your style will evolve, and it may take time to land on "the one" that sticks for the remainder of your ministry. What's most important is that your style is Holy-Spirit inspired, rather than attempts to sound like other preachers.

Harvesting Feedback

Many young preachers dream of standing ovations preceding every sermon. Let me burst that bubble out of the gate. To grow and become effective in converting and discipling souls, you need to hear positive, negative and constructive feedback. One of my most-memorable preaching experiences occurred at a local church as a seminary student. Reverend Daniels arranged for me to preach at a service where my classmates were present. I stepped to the podium, launched into my text and knew within minutes that I stank up the place. It was a miserable experience.

When I called Reverend Daniels, he asked, "So how did you feel about last night?"

"I'm not sure." Though I was afraid to hear his answer, I turned the question back to him.

He said, "Well, there was one good thing about how you handled it."

My heart jumped in hope at those words. *Thank you, God! He actually got something good out of that catastrophe!*

"What you did right, Daryl, is you did not hold us long. You saw that you were flunking, and you parachuted right out of there! I've seen preachers punish everyone by trying to rescue a sinking ship. You spared us that pain."

As I relived the humiliation, Pastor Daniels shared a deep truth that I will never forget.

"Don't worry about last night. That experience will do you more good than sermons that are home runs."

His words proved prophetic. In God's plan, nothing is wasted and this is true of sermon feedback.

Sermon feedback doesn't always come with the lightning speed of my horror story. Audience feedback can be highly valuable, but I caution you to approach its collection with great care. Pastor Daniels told me to avoid worrying about the reaction to a sermon while preparing it. While I recommend thinking about how to make your message clear and relatable, that is different from attempting to anticipate the reaction of the audience. For example, I don't suggest inserting pauses that prompt you to "pause for shouting here" like I have seen in preachers' notes. Let the Holy Spirit give you on-the-spot discernment about such things.

Before you deliver the message, ask God to give you an open mind about the reactions of parishioners and visitors. Some of the most-powerful sermons at Omega Church have been the ones where people were relatively quiet. My words were met by a thick, thoughtful silence as people sat reflecting. I could see some of them mouthing "Oh" as life applications became clear to them.

You cannot judge the success of a sermon by the volume of the audience. I asked students in a hermeneutics class if they ever indicated pleasure with an atrocious sermon. All of them raised a hand. To make a point, I then asked, "Why would your parishioners be any different?" Sometimes, people who make lots of noise are attempting to drown out their unpreparedness, stir up audience feedback or just amusing themselves.

While some sermons will elicit shouting and dancing, ensure every message includes motivations to make conscious changes. Whether you rely on storytelling or scriptural quotes, understand subdued responses are not always a cause for worry. If the listener is ever going to discuss what they've learned with a family member, friend or fellow believer, they need to internalize it.

The most-enlightening, timely feedback requires that you make yourself available via an informal receiving line after service. Vanessa and I have always made a point of joining everyone in the church vestibule as they interact. Some pastors depart the church or retreat to their office after preaching, missing a valuable opportunity. While we build bonds with all congregants and extend a personal welcome to visitors, we assess whether the sermon hit the bull's eye or fell short of the target.

You never know what types of responses you may get, but you can learn from all of them. Here are some popular ones and the associated takeaways:

1. "Pastor, I'm going to look at that Scripture again!" This response you want to hear most often. The message got the listener thinking and likely helped them see the scriptural passage in a new manner that could improve their life.

2. "Pastor, you were deep today!" This response usually merits a friendly follow-up to better understand what they are saying. It could mean they gained deep insight or your message soared far over their heads and missed the mark.

3. Silence. Be concerned when people talk to you about everything, but the sermon. This is not a case "where no news is good news." You want your message to make an impression that motivates feedback.

Pay attention to clusters of similar thoughts. Groupings of similar comments is often the best indicator of your sermon's performance. While your memories are fresh, reflect on these feedback conversations and interpret the "lessons learned" God embedded for you. I usually reflect alone—not relying on human counsel—but trusting in the guidance of the Holy Spirit. My prayer life helps me discern feedback to assess what worked, and the pitfalls that afflicted a sermon that landed with a thud.

If I summed up the most-common characteristic of sermons that generated negative feedback, it is failing to make the message plain. Refer to *Preparing Your Sermon Letter* (page 63) for strategies to avoid this catastrophe.

Taking Your Show on the Road

I cannot discuss the art of preaching without addressing preaching at churches other than your own. Preaching "on-the-road" presents opportunities to magnify and monetize your message, but you have far less room for error than when preaching at home.

I used to think that a pastor's relevance was determined by how many revivals he or she performed on the side. I pictured myself in such company: living with a packed bag at the door, traveling the country, conducting 30 revivals a year; administering my church by phone from hotel rooms. I experienced this life early in my ministry, especially when my work at United Theological Seminary expanded my national network. I traveled often, preaching the same sermons. Eventually, I asked myself, "What are you really accomplishing?"

As seminary executive responsibilities exposed me to leading ministers from across the country, I realized that many great road preachers had smaller churches that sometimes suffered from the absence of their shepherds. The more I observed in-demand guest preachers—of small, neglected churches or inspiring examples like Jeremiah Wright of Chicago's Trinity United Church of Christ, who preached far-and-wide while managing his church and tending to his congregation—the more I realized that only an elect few are called to conduct the critical balancing act required to regularly preach away from home.

Most pastors are called to put the needs of the congregation above their own. We will be judged by how we lead our people, and for most of us, that means performing leadership acts in person. An undeniable allure is built into most invitations to preach guest sermons. I am not suggesting that you don't take some of the opportunities presented. I counsel; however, that you consider such activities as infrequent "adventures" instead of an area of focus or heavy investment.

With over 30 years served at Omega, across multiple generations and phases of members' lives, nothing compares to the affect you can make for God at your home church. You face down the devil, fight for your congregation's spiritual health and see God reward your effort. Your effective leadership can reverberate throughout the church and community, outliving you in a way that you will never achieve with the most-crowd-pleasing guest sermon.

High Stakes

Paul instructed the young preacher to give himself wholly to his ministry gifts and live in a way that allowed his preaching and teaching to save himself and his hearers.

> *Do not neglect your gift, which was given you through prophecy when the body of elders laid their hands on you. Be diligent in these matters; give yourself wholly to them, so that everyone may see your progress. Watch your life and doctrine closely. Persevere in them, because if you do, you will save both yourself and your hearers.*
> —1 Timothy 4:14-16 NIV

This sobering reminder demonstrates the potential power of the gifts that God placed within you. As your pastoral journey develops, let the high stakes of ministry motivate you to rigorously prepare each sermon, collect feedback to improve the next one, honor God's call on your life with a commitment to authenticity and ensure that your focus prioritizes the spiritual care of your home congregation. Your pastoral experience will be full of highs, lows and perhaps even moments of monotony, but the principles shared helped me navigate the highest praise and the harshest criticisms.

Daryl Ward

Letter 6

Partnering with Your Spouse

Principle:
Your relationship with your spouse—as husband and wife and partners in ministry—makes a critical difference in your influence. Intentional partnering with your spouse bolsters your ability to lead your church and helps protect your marriage.

Dear Son,

God ratified my decision to marry the former Vanessa Oliver at many points in our marriage, but perhaps no more powerfully than when I was in my most weakened, vulnerable state. When I was deathly ill and written off for dead by the first set of doctors, Vanessa looked after me and advocated for me with every medical professional who crossed my path. Even when I was unable to process my surroundings, a peace driven by God's presence—and the work He was doing through my wife—filled me.

In the early weeks of my hospitalization, Vanessa was reminded that our stewardship extended beyond our marriage and family.

As he arrived to meet us at Cleveland Clinic, where he helped Vanessa place me for heightened care and analysis, the renowned pastor, Dr. Otis Moss, Jr., had a simple question for her: "What of the church?"

Vanessa was puzzled by the question, but Dr. Moss clarified that he was asking who would assume leadership of the church in my absence. Vanessa, who probably had not had a decent night's sleep in weeks, admitted that the question had not crossed her mind.

Dr. Moss, a slow, deliberate speaker, sharpened his point. "If you feel that you can, you should take over all pastoral responsibilities."

Although she was co-pastor, Vanessa hadn't seen herself taking over my duties while serving as my caretaker and health advocate. In light of what happened (refer to *Prayer is Fuel Letter* on page 23), Vanessa and I were grateful for Dr. Moss's counsel. She acted on his advice, and proved to be a highly-effective steward over a church grappling with whether I would be restored as their active pastor. No one could have been more trusted with Omega's well-being. Her leadership helped smooth my rehabilitation and recovery. I knew the one person most invested in my recovery, and in the continued prosperity of our congregation, held the reins. That removed a source of stress that I did not need.

The Incalculable Importance of a Complementary Spouse

Most people who have worked with or studied under Vanessa would agree that she is an exceptional woman. I can only claim partial credit for recognizing that early in our relationship. One of the things that drew me to her was the gifts she had that I did not. I am often credited for emotional intelligence, which is important, but I am amazed that God paired me with a brilliant wife. She speaks five languages and attended our undergraduate alma mater, The College of Wooster, on a major scholarship.

Early in our marriage, we recognized and leveraged the complementary nature of our gifts. When I was a student and director of seminary admissions, I found that Vanessa could help me organize and document the strategic thoughts and visions God bestowed on me. She is a linear thinker who likes to fill her calendars with check marks and lined-out items to prove that she "got things done." I, on the other hand, am not a numbers guy and I do not obsess over details. Vanessa is skilled at capturing critical information in reports and every letter is in its respective place.

While I benefit from Vanessa's administrative expertise, she defers to my people management skills. She admits that my ability to read people and reason with them has salvaged relationships with staff, ministers and officers who went on to mightily serve the church and advance its mission.

Neither Vanessa nor I would have accomplished as much as we have without one another. We have a clear view of the "headline" strengths God combined when He brought us together: her intelligence and drive, my wisdom and patience. The collective synergy deepened my comfort in our partnership and my abiding faith in God.

Preparing for Partnership

Whether you are married or dating a potential spouse, effective ministry partnerships don't just develop out of thin air. To set up yourself for a successful partnership, pray about how to embed the following practices and principles into your marriage or relationship:

1. Develop a shared commitment to pursue your individual God-given journeys.

   Vanessa's elevation to co-pastor may have surprised casual observers. Perhaps they mistook her for a typical "first lady," but I knew her gifts and spiritual calling. Growing up, she had no role models to indicate that a woman could become a respectable preacher or pastor. When we met in college, she believed her leadership skills and fluency in multiple languages aligned her with Peace Corps. She felt called to serve, but did not envision preaching.

   Neither Vanessa nor I entered marriage expecting to be pastors, much less co-pastors. We prospered in our respective evolutions because we jointly pursued God's direction for each professional step. Vanessa's call became increasingly spiritual as she encouraged and supported my transition from enterprising would-be attorney to full-time seminary student. Networking with my fellow students and seminary faculty deepened her sense of self and the ways in which God could use her talents.

   By the time I completed seminary, we relocated to Dayton, Ohio. Vanessa enrolled as a Christian education student at the seminary where I served as an administrator. A couple of years later, when I was appointed pastor of Omega Baptist Church, Vanessa applied her seminary training to establish a formal Christian education department. She introduced Vacation Bible School, and overhauled programming for Sunday school and Bible study. Vanessa's initiatives laid a solid foundation that accommodated Omega's explosive growth. Her strengths freed me to focus on preaching, teaching, officiating weddings, delivering eulogies and bonding with the congregation.

Those early years at Omega solidified our ability to recognize one another's gifts and operate with mutual respect. Vanessa said that this is where we learned how to live a passage from 1 Corinthians:

But in fact God has placed the parts in the body, every one of them, just as He wanted them to be. If they were all one part, where would the body be? As it is, there are many parts, but one body. The eye cannot say to the hand, "I don't need you!" And the head cannot say to the feet, "I don't need you!"
—1 Corinthians 12:18-21 NIV

The entirety of chapter 12 addresses the need for each part of the church body to respect the gifts and roles of others. The same applies to a Christian marriage and partnership. Marriages that collaborate in ministry work best when each spouse views the other's talents and gifts as opportunities, not as threats or competition. Pray daily to combat egos that block your ability to view spiritual growth and evolutions as exciting opportunities.

2. Let your spouse hear from God when doors open to new ministry opportunities, and when He wants you to influence the decision.

As you and your spouse encourage one another to walk with God, the specifics of your individual calls may change. This shift may introduce new ministry opportunities, and even the best opportunities can raise uncertainty and force difficult decisions. To keep a marriage strong throughout such periods, each spouse must surrender to God's expressed will, understanding that divining may require one spouse to counsel the other.

If not for Vanessa's counsel, I doubt I would have led Omega. We had been in Dayton two years when I received an invitation to serve as part-time pastor at the humble little church. While my primary obligation was Sunday-morning preaching, I was uncomfortable with the "opportunity." My hands were full running a first-of-its-kind Black Church Ministries program, and I moonlighted to make ends meet. Vanessa raised two children, while studying at the seminary. I aspired to become a pastor, but the timing did not feel right. I didn't want to further burden Vanessa and the children with my absence.

After preaching a guest sermon at Omega, Vanessa posed a question that spoke to my misgivings. Barely out of the parking lot, she turned to me and asked, "Daryl, could God be calling us to this church?" Her willingness to consider Omega's invitation marked a pivotal point in the decision-making process.

Vanessa's counsel influenced me to listen more closely to what God was saying than the objections raised by my earthly logic. She shared what she heard from God reflective of the type of give-and-take volley that characterized our respective ministry growth. She always acted out of desire to see me fulfill God's call on my life, and I reciprocated. As a result, God blessed our individual and collective collaborations.

3. Develop a shared resistance to conventional wisdom. Do not let what others say about the progression of your ministry shackle you.

   Whether how you share roles and responsibilities, or decisions about the direction, location or nature of your ministry, keep your focus on God's specific directions. Do not conform to societal norms and conventional wisdoms about how your ministry should look.

   Decades before Vanessa preached her first sermon, we encountered a woman who emphasized the extent to which God confounds conventional norms. We attended an event featuring Dr. Prathia Hall-Wynn of Philadelphia's Sharon Baptist Church. Amidst an audience of "Who's Who" of Rochester's Black preachers and community leaders, Dr. Wynn struck us as a barrier-breaking preacher. We had never experienced a highly-educated, refined, yet explosively powerful female pastor. Not only did this woman blow away the parishioners, she brought a group of initially resistant male pastors to their feet in fiery praise. Anointed.

   We were heavily affected in ways we didn't recognize at the time. Vanessa said that Dr. Wynn's example prepared her to preach. What once seemed a fantasy became plausible. Dr. Wynn's example prepared me to support Vanessa's call to preach and co-pastor. In a manner that transcended what I observed from mentors, it planted a seed to never oppose the call of any qualified woman. I credit this mindset for the fact that Omega's associate ministers are predominantly female. I am grateful for the ways God used Vanessa and me to mentor associates — male and female — who now pastor their own vibrant churches.

Freeing your partnership from demands of conventional wisdom includes discarding the idea that your respective ministry paths have to follow pre-ordained scripts. God is not necessarily calling you to complete seminary, pastor a "stepping stone" church and then shortly thereafter leave for a larger one, which you plan to grow to mega-church status. While seeking the Lord in the present, you never know His entire master plan.

Trust the uniqueness of the paths He designed for each of you, and the ways He unites you along those paths. Vanessa recommends couples in ministry, or preparing to enter such a partnership, be intentional about seeking God's call while investing in the health of the marriage. Be united atop the shared foundation of Holy Spirit guidance.

Characteristics of Healthy Partnerships

Consider these daily operating principles Vanessa and I use to help manage marriage and ministry.

1. While you serve each other as "help meets," don't look to your spouse in situations that only God can address.

   I received counsel in the earlier years of marriage that many pastors fail to reap the benefits of their spouse. I can't recall the speaker, but he said that when a spouse's advice is disregarded, we "fight what God gave to help us." Whenever Vanessa and I have heated conversations, I reflect on this counsel and the biblical phrase "help meet." And as she likes to remind me, "I am not your enemy. I am trying to help."

   Reminding myself of her good intentions helps me consider her suggestions and appreciate her contributions with humility.

And the Lord God said, "It is not good that the man should be alone; I will make him an help meet for him."
—Genesis 2:18

This reference to the help meet God intended for Adam when creating Eve tells me that He provided Vanessa as my equal with mutually-beneficial attributes.

As important as it is to serve one another, be aware of limits that humanity places on each partner. I took some challenges straight to God and awaited His inspiration. For example, the transition into retirement. After Vanessa and I announced our official retirement date, her schedule remained full running Omega Community Development Corporation. I, on the other hand, had a comparably blank slate, which provided time to write this book.

Adjusting from a calendar packed with administrative meetings, sermon preparation and community appearances, to a cleared calendar has been difficult. I often issue prayers that boil down to "What's next?" God showed me it was time for a new generation of leadership to help ensure Omega's relevance in a rapidly changing world, but that knowledge hasn't made the transition easy. While I have Vanessa's emotional support, I have not burdened her with advising me through it. It is God's job to direct me toward, and through, the next phase of my life.

I take advantage of the increased discretionary time to listen for His guidance while serving Vanessa more-directly than ever. I prepare and serve dinner for her each night. While she's making things happen in an important, stressful job, I try to keep a clean, neat home and ensure she has what she needs. I consider it an honor.

Vanessa graciously accepts my contributions, and has a similar perspective about the type of help she accepts from me. She said, "I am in this role [running Omega Community Development Corporation] not because I am the pastor's wife, but because God told me to do it. I would never have chosen this on my own. Because He told me to do this, I look to Him to provide what I need to prosper, not Daryl."

It takes conversation to make sure we are aligned. Keeping mutual help-meet expectations realistic and specific has been an important characteristic of our partnership.

2. Manage conflict with open communication and an understanding of who is making the final call.

    One of the best ways to ensure that you get through conflicts with your partnership intact is to draw clear "swim lanes" that spell out who will be the final authority on decisions. When it came to co-pastoring responsibilities, Vanessa deferred to me on church matters on which we disagreed.

    She said, "I defer to you because Omega hired Daryl Ward to be its pastor, not me." She worked with me to define her areas of responsibility so that she could, in her words, stay in her lane. She enjoyed the ability to place the thorny management challenges in my lap!

    This submission doesn't mean my wife is a shrinking violet. Vanessa gives her opinion, whether I want it or not. I appreciate her willingness to speak her mind, and the thoughtful way she shares her opinion when I am able to hear and consider it. Even in cases where our disagreements are passionate and I assert my authority over an area she directly manages, I respect her opinion and weigh it before making the final call. She has proven right too many times for me to do otherwise. It's not uncommon for me to overrule her preference initially, and then scrutinize the situation closely. If I see evidence supporting her advised course of action, I'm not afraid to reverse my decision.

3. As important as it is to thoughtfully manage conflict, do not fall into the trap of sacrificing what is best for the church just to get along with your spouse.

   Managing conflict in your partnership is important because it can endanger your church or ministry. You may be tempted to use church business or politics as a way to "make peace" with your spouse after a nasty disagreement. As partners in ministry, it helps to agree that church-related conflicts will be decided by Holy Spirit guidance and the deciding party's sense of what is best for the ministry. If your marriage is experiencing challenges, address them without letting them affect your ministry responsibilities. It's healthy to deal with relationship conflicts in the context of your home rather than on the job.

   While you need to protect the church from the effect of marital disagreements or stressors, make sure to invest in the health of your marriage. When Vanessa accepted her call to preach, she visited with Dr. H. Beecher Hicks of Washington D.C.'s Metropolitan Baptist Church. He counseled Vanessa that though she would remain a committed wife and mother, she had to put her call first. When he sensed her surprise, he reassured her that did not mean her relationships with me nor the children should suffer.

   "Do you think God didn't know you were married when He called you?" While pursuing her role as co-pastor would limit the amount of daily time she could spend with us, Dr. Hicks encouraged her to trust God's help in protecting these critical relationships.

For Vanessa and me, our faith in God's desire to protect our marriage motivates us to spend focused time away from the church. We like to commune over a good meal, and take vacations that allow us to escape co-pastor bonds for a few days. I remind her that we are more than co-workers by surprising her with an unexpected bouquet of flowers or carefully chosen clothing from the clearance racks at Von Maur, our favorite local department store. Look for opportunities, whether an hour or a week, to leave work and connect with your spouse.

No magic checklist about how to protect your marital and family health exists. I suggest engaging your spouse in conversation to compare notes. Are the two of you spending enough time together away from church? Are you spending consistent time connecting with your children? Are you spending ministry time on tasks or responsibilities that are driven by habit rather than necessity? Think through your answers, and pray about what actions to take. I credit this self-examination for the ways God blessed our ministry and our family.

4. Trust that God will be glorified when you and your spouse coordinate the development and communication of your partnership.

Pursuing a co-pastoring arrangement or any relationship in which spouses share leadership roles can be tricky. Especially for relationships that evolve publicly, in the way that Vanessa's and mine did. Naysayers are always looking to second-guess a spouse's elevation or changes in leadership structure. Instead of worrying about these individuals, trust that those with good intentions will be best served when you stay in sync with how your partnership operates.

A good example is the way in which Vanessa and I handled the early years of co-pastoring. Vanessa summed up our approach as follows: "In cases where the male is the lead or the 'original' pastor, the male ego sometimes has to be humbled to communicate your partnership to the church. Daryl has such humility, his ego doesn't need to be stroked much. That's probably why he had no problem helping the congregation appreciate my gifts. The husband in a ministry partnership needs to give thought to this because the historical model has always been a male leader. Making room for a female leader requires intentionality in messages and action. You can do that without saying, 'Hey, make room for my wife,' but Daryl modeled how to show respect for a wife's ministry gifts and contributions."

While I worked to make room for Vanessa to contribute as co-pastor, once the door opened, she earned the adoration and admiration of the congregation with her work ethic and Spirit-powered application of her talents. Her professional transition taught me the value of supporting your spouse's evolution as a gradual, incremental process. As your spouse's role in ministry grows, be aware that they shouldn't necessarily take new responsibilities in leaps and bounds. Let them prove themselves one-step at a time.

Whether you are the one whose role is changing most dramatically, commit with your spouse to seek God about how to support one another and set up each other for success. I always approached Vanessa's transformation as my wife and my jewel. As she walked in God's will, my job was to follow the Holy Spirit's direction and support what God was doing. We spent years setting the course of Vanessa's transition and our division of duties. The planning was especially important to our congregation's ability to respect and trust what we were doing. Vanessa points out that this work is hard, but necessary. This type of work was likely neglected in infamous cases of co-pastor relationships that were extensions of what seemed trendy.

Thoughts for Those Still Seeking Your Partner
If you are awaiting the mate that God has for you, evaluate potential spouses with the foregoing points in mind. When encountering someone with whom you have romantic chemistry, a shared faith and similar values, raise the stakes. Look beyond the physical chemistry because as a wise man once said, "Love grows, lust wilts."

Is this someone with a vibrant relationship with Christ? Are they adventurous enough to support the evolution of your ministry? Can they grow with you? Do they possess strengths and capabilities that you do not? Do you view them as an equal? Do they handle conflict in ways consistent with principles shared in this letter? You will not find a roadmap to the perfect partnership, but you need a partner who shares the majority of traits addressed here.

As you seek your spouse, pray diligently. It will not be easy to evaluate which person aligns with the markers of a soul mate with whom you can also chart an adventurous ministry career. You will need Holy Spirit-powered insight for this project, so don't forsake your power source. When I was ready to find a wife, I spent so much time praying about her that it became second nature.

A Way of Life, Not a Path

A minority of pastors will have their spouse join as co-pastor, and many spouses may not likely enter full-time ministry. Your marriage—and any ministry partnership shared with your spouse—will be distinct from my experiences with Vanessa. I do know; however, that your marriage and ministry has the best opportunity to thrive when you recognize and coordinate the use of your complementary gifts, embrace a flexible sense of adventure about where God's call may lead you and respectfully address conflict using a pre-ordained decision-making process. A way of life driven by these principles will enrich your church, your marriage and your family through the twists and turns of your unique path.

Letter 7

Your Support System: Family and Friends

Principle:
When you invest in family relationships and friends whom God weaves into your life, you will be more equipped for success in ministry. The unique privileges of leadership come with risks that require discernment to identify the friends on whom you can lean. Today's investments in relationships with your spouse, children and close relatives will pay dividends in the future.

Dear Son,
Leadership can be a lonely place, but trust God to place unshakeable family and friends in your life. They may not always be who you would have chosen, but pay close attention: they are there for a reason. As God blesses your ministry, you will reach into new and higher echelons in your local community, and potentially regional and national levels. You will have to determine how to use this God-given power and influence. Do not use it for selfish gain, and avoid

people who would try to use you for access to it. Instead, take time to develop a family-and-friend network that helps you navigate the challenges and trappings of pastoral leadership.

The investment in family relationships starts with spousal and parent-child relations. Refer to *Partnering with Your Spouse Letter* (page 87) for the former. Investing in relationships with your children requires acknowledging the unique challenges that pastors face when parenting.

Parenting: An Awesome Call in its Own Right

Several powerful principles played a significant role in my development. I grew up in a loving, two-parent household in Mt. Healthy, Ohio, outside Cincinnati. When my parents relocated us there from downtown Cincinnati, we were among the first African American families in the area. While challenging aspects of being the first wave of children to integrate the local schools existed, my parents committed to placing my sister and me in a progressive, demanding educational system. Because they valued our participation in institutions run by African-Americans, active membership at a church in Avondale provided balance to our predominantly white school.

While my mother worked at a Greyhound Bus station, my father earned the majority of the household income as manager of a grocery store. He was a humble man, but I never thought about his social status or earning power as a child. I looked up to him because he was wise, fair, made sure the bills were paid and ensured we had a home.

My father was the first person to push me towards manhood. He expected the best out of me, which motivated me.

The first time he told me that he was proud of me I was a grown man. The apparent expression of shock on my face caused him to say, "I have been [proud of you] for a long time, but I couldn't tell you before now."

He spent my childhood and college years molding, shaping and pushing me. I imagine that disclosing his pride too early would have contradicted the humility he had modeled for me. He died in his early fifties, but he lived a powerful example that positioned me to hear, accept and act on God's call on my life.

My father's example has a special resonance; especially as an African American male. In a time where most children are reared in single-parent homes, some have lost sight of the role fathers play in their children's prosperity. Stories and methods of ambitious, complicated fathers like Earl [Tiger] Woods, Joseph [Michael] Jackson and Richard [Venus and Serena] Williams should be captured and shared for all parents to review. These men pushed their children to heights unforeseen in their professions. For every one of these figures, hundreds of thousands of fathers likewise powered the emergence of Black doctors, lawyers, entrepreneurs, engineers and professionals from every possible field.

A mother's presence makes the greatest contribution to a child's healthy development. My mother was not just a loving, devoted figure who kept a clean home and fed us well. She was a woman of strong opinions who had a gift for speaking her mind. No wonder I grew up to be a pastor who supports the rights and abilities of female preachers. Most of all, my mother was my protector. I never had to question whether she was looking out for me.

My mother laid the foundation of my development while my father contributed in ways that only a responsible male parent can. In my experience, a father who has his act together is second-to-none in wanting to maximize a child's potential. My father often communicated his desire for my success. When he died, I realized he had been the only man who considered my success as a victory for himself. He loved me and mentored me as if his life depended on it. His urging was not for my sake only because he motivated me to pursue goals that considered others' welfare.

Parenting Principles

If God blessed you with the privileges and challenges of parenting, rear your children with the same reverence you bring to stewarding your church. The following principles were derived from my parents' example and strategies Vanessa and I used to balance the leadership of Omega with oversight of our children:

1. Embrace sacrifice.

    Looking after your children's development will require you to set aside other priorities. If you cannot avoid a scheduling conflict between an administrative meeting and a critical parent-teacher conference, have the church meeting proceed without you. If your child is in crisis or requires your attention during an especially hectic week, have an associate deliver that week's sermon.

    After my father's death, my mother told me of the irony she observed during my college study abroad in Spain. When my father learned that I ran out of money, he threw on a ratty, worn coat he should have long since upgraded and trekked to the credit union. His attire spoke to his tightness with a dollar, but he cracked open his precious savings account to aid me. I hold his hike as a memory of the quiet, humble strength that drove his sacrificial efforts to challenge and support me.

2. Teach humility.

Today's parents seem to shower their children with endless praise. Gold stars and affirming pronouncements are awarded for doing what was expected when I was a child. While my mother mixed her assignment of chores and around-the-house responsibilities with clear evidence of her love, I wasn't sure that my father liked me until I was in college.

I was home for the summer, working at a Kroger's grocery store. Because my father managed another branch, I often ran into people who worked with him.

I met co-workers who knew about my schooling and various accomplishments. Whenever I asked how they knew so much about me, they credited my father. "He talks about you all the time. He is so proud of you!"

This revelation was shocking because my father had erred on the side of keeping me humble. He provided for me, set a positive example and challenged me to meet standards of behavior and character. He instilled the humility in me as a child, then took time to express his affirmation and validation as I became a man. You will find your own way of balancing those two important phases, but be mindful to instill humility in your children.

Your status as a pastor or Christian leader provides a unique opportunity to model humility before your children. When a new acquaintance asks how I preferred to be addressed, I say, "My mother named me Daryl, and if that was good enough for her we can go with that." Unless relevant to the context, addressing me as "Doctor" or "Senior Pastor" is not necessary. That's why few people know I earned a juris doctorate in law.

Years ago, I stopped wearing a suit and tie every Sunday and I only wear pastoral robes on special occasions. Leadership does not require putting out the most hot air. I don't need to be the center of attention to have God-ordained influence and I appreciate the opportunity to publicly model these behaviors for my children.

3. Enforce discipline.

Disciplining is not the part of parenting longed for when anticipating a baby's arrival, swaddling them in blankets or rocking them to sleep on your chest. You will soon be reminded that parenting is a J-O-B. Parenting is not a plaything or a lighthearted experience provided for your amusement. Your job is to prepare your children for the world. Giving them everything they ask, or letting them get away with misdeeds does not prepare them for the realities of how the world works.

As a parent, do your job to the best of your ability so your children develop into successful citizens, and dedicated Christians. As unpleasant as it can feel, discipline is important. When your children engage in sinful, disrespectful or disobedient behavior, remember that correcting and penalizing them is a healthy part of their maturation. Just make sure that you are applying principles and methods consistent with relevant scriptural examples.

4. Seek God's inspiration about when to share sensitive or complicated truths.

   For years, I didn't understand my mother's habitual saying, "Stay out of grown folks' conversations." Whenever friends or family sat around the kitchen table, she sent me out of the room. Later, I learned she protected me from some complicated realities for which I was not ready. When she revealed some of these facts to me in adulthood, I understood her logic. One of the more striking examples involved my father's identity.

   On family trips to Georgia, my father's friends and relatives addressed him as JP. Given that his name was Lester, the nickname was odd. Whenever I asked my mother about it, she waved away the question. Years later, I learned that my father had initially not been raised by his biological father. His mother chose to name him for an uncle of his, James Preston. For most of his childhood, he was raised by my grandmother and her family as "JP."

His mother passed away while he was a minor. Though his grandmother continued raising him, she contacted her grandson's biological father, Lester Ward. She informed him that the child he left behind lost his mother. I don't know why my grandfather had not been in my father's life, but once he knew my father's mother died, he stepped up and did the right thing. Not only did he drive to Georgia and retrieve JP to live in Cincinnati with his wife and children, my grandfather legally changed my father's name to Lester Ward, Junior. Tears spring to my eyes when I tell that story. Learning those truths about my father's origins carried much weight based on when I learned them. Likewise, as your children mature, be mindful of those truths that you should let them grow into before sharing.

5. Let them fall, but always pick them up.

    During those college summers at Kroger's, I worked a 3:00 pm to midnight shift. On occasion, store management tapped my shoulder and told me to go home an hour early. Happy to be released, I called home to let me my father know I was ready for a ride. He always said, "I'll be there shortly," but he didn't mean it! He sat on his couch and finished watching whatever show he had on before heading out.

    I paced, resenting his "nerve." How dare he leave me waiting? As only a hotheaded young man can, I fantasized all sorts of brave things to say to him when he arrived.

Years later, I considered those incidents and placed myself in my father's shoes. He received calls to serve as my "Uber driver" at the end of a long workday. He had probably arrived home within the hour and barely had time to eat dinner before seeking a rare hour of relaxation in front of the television. His wearying schedule included a midnight run to get me, not an hour earlier. Thank God I had the good sense to leave all those hot-headed thoughts unspoken! That would not have ended well for me.

This story sums up a parent's call to provide for their children, while helping them understand that the world does not revolve around them. While he taught me about manhood, responsibility and humility, my father never left any doubt that he was there for me. Just like those nights when I paced Kroger's, whether he came when I thought he should, he always picked me up. Sacrifice for your children. Model humility, enforce discipline, and make sure they know you will always support them.

Your Children and Your Church

Because you need to be present for your children and spend time at church, establish your church as a suitable second home for them. Think of your pastoral office as the cocoon in which they can spend evenings and weekends. When you manage your church with integrity, influencing your children to think of church as home will benefit them for years to come.

Allow your children to play in your office whether you are hosting guests or not. As a young minister, I thought it was unprofessional to have children playing in a pastor's office. As I aged, I realized that while visiting ministers and guests should be welcome, *they* are the intruders in your office. The kids are at home!

To avoid the infamous pastor's kids (PK) syndrome, train up your children as everyday kids, not PKs with assumed privileges and entitlement. The outside world—and sometimes church members—will place unwelcomed pressures by holding your children to higher standards than they set for their own. Such pressures and extra attention are unfair. They can threaten children's spiritual and emotional development. Don't add to it.

One way to counter these pressures is to resist efforts to treat your children differently from their church peers. Do not have birthday parties for them at church unless that same honor is extended to all children. Don't allow them to be elevated above other children. Let them fit in with all the other kids. Inevitably, some members will pay them special attention, but do not encourage it.

Reverend Daniels said, "Raise your children so someone else can love them!" Loving and accepting them as they are, while working hard to protect them from PK pressures, helps produce loveable children.

As you work to foster equal treatment for your children and their peers, follow the same standard at home. Each child is unique and needs to be parented as such. Love on each of them equally. My mother taught me not to show more love for one child over another, even if the ways in which that love is communicated differs by child.

When communicating your love with financial support—weekly allowances, after-school activity funding or back-to-school clothing budgets—spend approximately the same amount of money on each of them. It may hurt at times, but because it is measurable, it will pay off later. You may have to do more for one child because of an emergency or special circumstance, but keep track so that a similar favor can be given to the other children at the appropriate time.

A Pleasant Surprise

As I wrote this letter, all three of our children had returned to Dayton to raise their families and pursue God's purpose. This pleasant surprise blessed us as many of our children's peers—who also graduated with advanced degrees—put down roots in larger cities. They have no plans to return to Dayton.

When asked to explain our children's enthusiasm for their hometown, I credited the Omega Church family. Our members loved our children unconditionally and let them grow into who God made them to be. They helped make the church an extension of home. Our children internalized the church office as home away from home; where they were always welcomed without judgment, pressure or preferential treatment. While I haven't asked all of them about it, their returning to worship among (and in Joshua's case, lead) a body of believers who spent years investing in their welfare is not a coincidence.

The Precious Commodity of Friendship

> "A true leader has the confidence to stand alone, the courage to make tough decisions, and the compassion to listen to the needs of others. He doesn't set out to be a leader, but becomes one by the quality of his actions and the integrity of his intent. In the end, leaders

are much like eagles...they do not flock; you find them one at a time."
—Unknown

Family relationships are critical for spiritual leaders because we do not often have a wealth of close friendships. Rigorous demands leave little space for fraternizing, and when leisure time is available, be selective about whom you involve.

Reverend Daniels taught me to avoid making fellow pastors the heart of my social circle. "It's not good for preachers to run in a pack," he said. Having observed such packs in the years since his godly advice, I understand his rationale. Too often, following group rules takes priority over following God's call for each preacher and his/her congregation.

Having said that, developing systematic interaction with your peers in ministry can be healthy. Omega Church joined a local organization, West Dayton Caravan, a few years ago. This monthly gathering of pastors allowed me to spend quality time with fellow seminary-educated, ecumenical leaders who push their congregations to make a positive influence in the community. Their worship style is progressive and relevant to today's worshipper. We collaborate for Easter and other holiday services, jointly host summer learning programs for youth and administer annual scholarship programs.

While I also have monthly American Baptist Association meetings, I find special benefit in my Caravan fellowship because we face similar ministry challenges. The majority of my ABA colleagues lead white suburban churches whose communities and members require different priorities and ministry approaches. In some ways, I find it difficult to share what's going on in my life and ministry with them. On the other hand, at times I feel free to be more transparent with the ABA colleagues. Encounters with them during monthly meetings create a "safe space" where I can sometimes let down my guard.

As you develop relationships with fellow pastors, keep in mind the difference between mentors and friends. Reliable mentors are necessary, but they are not necessarily your friends. Attentive, in-demand pastors are usually too busy to "pal around." Value every moment you get with them as a learning opportunity; not a social exchange. I rarely spent in-person time with the most important mentors in my ministry. Most often we communed via phone and discussions focused on specific topics or challenges I faced. God may provide you with mentors who evolve into close friends, but to maximize the value of each mentoring relationship, do not start out expecting that.

The Power of a Family Foundation

Thinking back to my days as a young minister, I imagine that you may be asking, "What do I do when I feel lonely?" In my experience, God always took care of such needs. He delivered that relief in many ways:

- The unpredictable counsel of a beloved member of Omega
- The opportunity for a restful vacation with Vanessa
- Exposure to a nourishing sermon delivered by another preacher
- Fellowship with an insightful ministry colleague

I never knew how He would provide for me in those lonely moments, but my family was often a key source of solace. As a leader, you need to rely on family for emotional support. God can and will send friends from multiple sources, but these individuals will be quite rare. In this line of work, you meet many people who turn out to be fair-weather friends. They are there for you only as long as they think you can offer them something in return. Relying on just anyone for friendship and support can set you up for frequent disappointment. That is why I value establishing family as my first, most-reliable layer of support.

Choosing your family as the most-important earthly support system reinforces the need to cultivate solid relationships with your spouse and children. When a health crisis robbed me of the ability to preach or lead Omega Church, Vanessa led a small team of family and trusted associates to protect the church: financially and operationally. I was free to focus on my recovery.

I am thankful for the dramatic manner God demonstrated the value of family and carefully selected friends. Invest in these relationships on a daily basis, drawing parenting inspiration from your elders and mentors and praying for discernment as God reveals new friends to you. Maintaining your focus will protect not only you, but your church and each congregant you serve.

Letter 8

Time Management

Principle:
Think of time management as an external form of stewardship that comes with leadership responsibilities. Managing how you spend your time can benefit members of your congregation, and the church as an institution. Benefits of time management are rooted in the spiritual growth and ministry skills that God unveils when you make yourself more available to Him.

Dear Son,

Although time management is embedded in the other letters, I dedicated a letter to it because it is critical to your effectiveness as pastor or leader. Without effective time management, you won't be able to fulfill day-to-day demands of administration, commitments to family and your spiritual enrichment. The growth and success of a church is limited—or expanded—by its pastor. A pastor who has not mastered time management will restrain growth to fit within personal limitations. It is crucial that you "order your steps" to have adequate time to seek God for inspiration.

God is in charge of every fraction of a second and can use any experience to enrich your ministry effectiveness. Let His sovereignty motivate you to think strategically about how to invest the one commodity that cannot be bought, reused or stored: time. Consider these examples from my journey:

- When in college, I played a DJ. I hosted *Daryl's Jazz* on the school's radio station. I enjoyed the experience, but when I aired the final show, I was certain it would be my last time doing anything in radio. Years later; however, I hosted *Black Impact*, a weekly program featured on Dayton's most-popular African-American radio station. As I exposed tens of thousands of listeners to interviews with leading politicians, activists and intellectuals, God blessed Omega Baptist Church with unique credibility in the community. I am forever grateful for the unexpected byproduct Omega received from broadcasting experience I amassed years prior.
- During my college tenure, I was also involved in theatrical arts including a role in *Raisin in the Sun*. As with radio, I engaged in theater with no intention of pursuing it as a profession, yet a flair for the theatrical proved to be a major influence for Omega. From captivating the City of Dayton with professionally produced Easter services at UD Arena, to our pioneering dance ministry, to high-quality Black History and other holiday programs and plays, I

revisited observations acquired during those college years.

- A year out of college, I learned foundational leadership and office management principles on which I still rely. While in law school, I served as an intern in the Office of the Dean of Students. I observed behaviors that were useful in leadership positions at Colgate Rochester and United Theological seminaries. On a lighter note, working in the office also helped me develop a taste for black coffee, which fueled me through long hours of sermon preparation and administrative meetings.

- This next pivotal example occurred when I accepted the call to preach. Within weeks, I had a stunning meeting with Dr. H. Beecher Hicks, the very pastor under whom I heard God speak. He advised me to leave Washington D.C. and Georgetown Law School, and enroll in seminary in Rochester.

His counsel did not make sense. With one year of law school to complete, I planned to earn my degree while serving at the elbow of a pre-eminent pastor (in November 1993, *Ebony Magazine* honored Dr. Hicks as one of "The Fifteen Greatest African-American Preachers"). But as Dr. Hicks shared, I had to accept that God had a different path for me.

Because I obeyed what I heard as the voice of God embedded in Dr. Hicks' counsel, I arrived at the seminary just as the school's director of admissions was leaving. I was appointed interim director of recruitment and assistant to the provost, Dr. Leonard Sweet. The income helped pay off my Georgetown student debt while completing school from afar, and I discovered that I had skill for admissions and recruitment. Helping turn the department around earned Leonard's trust. By the time he was hired to serve as president of United Theological Seminary, he asked me to join his staff in Dayton. If I had taken the conventional route about how to spend my time and remained in Washington, I may have missed the opportunity to work with some of the most-innovative pastors in the country, or reach the doorsteps of Omega.

Because how you spend time plays a big role in your ministry, it's worthwhile to consider time management from strategic and tactical perspectives.

Strategic Principles of Time Management

1. Ensure that a significant percentage of time is spent investing in your members.

   I read that a great pastor is not measured by how many times his or her name is published in the paper, but by how many of the flock are noticed and appreciated in the world. Thus, my greatest joy comes from seeing Omega members prosper outside the walls of the church. When I see founders of thriving businesses who are generous faith-based philanthropists, godly physicians who selflessly serve low-income patients and determined educators who exemplify Christ while fighting the odds to aid at-risk children, I know Omega is fulfilling God's vision. A church does not achieve its mission based on the brilliance of its pastor, but based on the aggregated toil of its people. While the size of your church will require some delegation of this responsibility, God wants you to equip each member with tools to positively influence their home, work and community. This directive is how we accomplish God's work.

I learned early in pastoral ministry to filter decisions about time management through the principle that I prefer to bloom where I am planted. Your priorities should include direct connections with members about their spiritual journeys, teaching Bible study, maintaining focus at home and collaborating with associate ministers, ministry leaders and board members.

Consistent time invested with members and leadership cements relationships that count in the end. As of this writing, the senior housing development is under construction on the Harvard Campus, as well as the Hope Center for Families. I am humbled to realize the effort Vanessa and I invested to build spiritual and professional mentoring relationships, resulted in volunteers and leaders who work to make these projects a reality. When I consider the fruits of investments in members' development, I rest easy knowing that I chose those relationships over the potential renown associated with extra-curricular activities.

2. Take every free moment captive for study and reflection.

   Appreciate that every moment is a gift from God and treat each moment with that in mind. While you need to schedule time for study and reflection, this activity is so important that it should be your "go-to" whenever time opens in your schedule. Time set aside for study will often be crowded by unpredictable family events, administrative emergencies or other developments. Never assume that you'll have time to study later. When time is available to study and enrich your understanding of the Word, take it.

3. Cultivate a diverse body of reading material.

   An effective pastor is a well-rounded one. It pays to interact with people from various lifestyles, within your church and as you move throughout your community. While it is important to stay current on the latest scholarship about church administration, exegetical material and theology, don't neglect publications about world affairs, local and state current events and popular culture. I like to read a good novel when I can.

4. Set timelines and plans built on patience.

   One aspect of time management is developing timelines that provide estimations of how long it will take to achieve goals. If you never make plans, what assurance do you have of accomplishing goals?

   Keep in mind that not all goals will be accomplished according to estimates or expectations. Sometimes God gives a vision that will not happen as you envisioned. Consider King David who desired to build God's temple; however, his role was to provide resources for his son, Solomon, to fulfill the task.

Take time to evaluate activities on your calendar, and the progress made on them. Sometimes things run behind schedule because of mistakes, but oftentimes, God is calling you to be patient. In these cases, remember that good things often take time to develop, while successes that happen with a snap of the finger can evaporate just as quickly.

For example, years before it materialized, I had a vision of Omega's security team helping worshippers cross Salem Avenue, the busy thoroughfare on which the church sets. The Jewish congregation that originally owned the property offered this service, and it did not take long for me to develop the same aspiration. The vision alone wasn't enough because we needed God to send the right people. As we experienced rapid increases in membership, we did not have volunteers with the right mix of professional security experience, leadership skills and time to provide this service.

Enough time passed making it easy to abandon this vision; however, as I look at our dedicated security team today, I thank God that His visions do not come with expiration dates! If your attempts to implement a vision aren't working, don't assume the vision is ill-fated. Seek the Lord about it. Until God tells you otherwise, keep trying. Even your misses count.

Tactical Tips

Certain strategic principles can apply to an unpredictable number of scenarios and challenges you will encounter. Combined with simple, specific observations I gathered over three decades in ministry, the following tips may be of best use if you're new to this "pastoring thing:"

1. When visiting members at the hospital, a little bit goes a long way.

    Visiting sick-and-shut-in members is an important pastoral duty, but in most every case, it is best to make your visit brief. Most sick people need rest, and often benefit from quality time with family and friends.

    I did not understand this principle until I endured extensive hospitalization and rehabilitation. While I was grateful for visitors, I often felt trapped by those who did not know when to leave.

    As you settle into a seat next to your parishioner, pray for discernment, check a clock, set your estimated departure time and stick to it. Your presence and prayer for healing will brighten a patient's day by confirming you and the church care about them.

2. You get credit just for "passing through."

    Someone told me about pastoring by passing through. Without question, your members need to see you in places other than the pulpit. However, with the exception of those needing your physical participation to succeed, you don't have to attend every Bible study or church social event. Be aware of what is happening, but in most cases, all you need to do is stop through long enough to greet participants. People know you are busy; so you get credit for being there albeit brief.

3. Limit the time spent in administrative meetings.

   Don't run yourself ragged trying to attend every board meeting. I try to attend meetings where the committee may be in crisis or working on a critical project. I prioritize newly-established committees by attending the first few gatherings. The intent is to help define the agenda and ensure the primary objectives align with the church's mission and priorities. Once accomplished, my ongoing presence is not needed.

   You can save yourself lots of administrative time by modeling qualities for your staff and board to emulate—a consistent work ethic and integrity. When your leadership team exhibits these qualities, you are empowered to spend more time on ministry.

4. You're not a Human Resources officer.

   You need to be involved in every staff hiring; however, you only need to own the process when hiring a CFO (business manager) and minister of music.

   I hired a business manager without applying the John Maxwell "friendship" principle noted in the *Administration Letter* (page 35). According to Maxwell, hiring should include an assessment of whether the individual is someone whose company you could enjoy in agreement or conflict. When I hired solely based on the strength of the candidate's resume, it led to a miserable experience for everyone.

If the business manager is your most-important behind-the-scenes hiring decision, the minister of music is probably your highest-profile one. That fact influenced me twice to step back from the hiring process and let the committee select and conduct interviews through a professional, nationwide search. The short tenures of both employees left me wishing I had ensured no one was hired without interviewing with me in person.

For sensitive positions, you need individuals who can disagree without being disagreeable, and whose hearts are clear so you can trust their counsel and judgment. Candidates who don't pass this test must be bypassed.

5. Let the office staff do its job.

    Don't let micro-management of non-financial staff eat your time. Support and affirm your staff publicly to make their jobs easier, but when performance problems are encountered, chastise them professionally and privately. Don't get so concerned with whether everyone is doing their job that you neglect aspects of yours. Set an example and give everyone the chance to follow it.

6. Make yourself available, but protect your time.

    Some might call me crazy, but I never limit the scope of activities I support on behalf of my members. I serve as the first option for counseling, as well as handling weddings and funerals. I work for God, and He charged me to study His Word and serve His people. As such, the only boundaries that determine whether I counsel a parishioner, perform a wedding or preach a eulogy are other pastoral commitments.

A skilled, trustworthy administrative assistant makes all the difference. I have that in Theresa Buycks, who has served Omega in this critical role for decades. Theresa knows me so well, she drafts correspondences more-effectively than I can. As the first point of contact for people requesting my time, she acts as gatekeeper and protects me. While at times I overrule her instincts to accept emergency requests, it is a blessing to have her protecting my calendar. I appreciate the ways we look out for one another.

Considering the last two points reinforce the importance of your office staff, express your appreciation for their efforts. As nonprofit entities, most churches can never pay their employees what they are worth in the general marketplace. Don't let that stop you from praying for inspiration about ways to show respect and reward efforts. I have always insisted that we pay our staff reliably. Through various staff reductions and across-the-board pay cuts, which affected Vanessa and me, Omega never missed a payroll. While it's not enough on its own, it helps communicate our appreciation for faithful staff.

Don't Let Time Pass You By

Applying strategic thought to how you invest time helps maximize your ability to use unique gifts in service to the individuals God called us to pastor. Seeking God's guidance to ensure focus on the duties to which He called you, provides time to commune with Him and develop maturity necessary to work your calling. Protecting time also makes room for life experiences that can pay long-term, often unexpected, dividends for the churches and nonprofits you lead.

Letter 9

Protect Yourself:

Morality and Integrity

Principle:

As a pastor or spiritual leader, expect to face temptations geared to your most-distinct weaknesses. Protect your morality and integrity by proactively contrasting what tempts you with what you value most by regularly assessing your habits and testing your loyalties. The rewards of a moral life powered by integrity can bless you, your family, congregation and community you serve.

Dear Son,

The Merriam-Webster online dictionary defines integrity as "firm adherence to a code of especially moral or artistic values." The stakes inherent in your ability to live according to such a code are high. After all, the greatest impediment to the next visitor entering your sanctuary is not a competing church. More often, potential worshippers are turned away by high-profile and grassroots examples of pastoral immorality and hypocrisy. Non-believers and lapsed Christians point to the "wall of shame" as a reason to avoid church. What preventive steps can be taken to minimize—better, yet, eliminate—joining the ranks of the fallen?

The precursor to self-destruction is temptation. Discussing temptation requires slowing down to assess personal habits that can increase vulnerability or be stumbling blocks to observers. Analyzing your habits and temptations helps protect morality and integrity. Doing the pre-work to safeguard personal conduct—and its impact on churches or ministries—honors God's call and His plans for the institutions you lead.

It's Not Your Fault: Temptation is Real

Don't be upset when temptations come and you are tempted by them. The enemy uses stealth tactics to ensnare you and you're human! The test is how you respond to temptations. I faced my share of temptations and avoided most of them, which I credit to listening to the Holy Spirit. In every case, that thing I wanted so badly turned out to be "not so hot," while those the Lord told me to cherish proved incredible.

Let's review those visceral, "crucible" moments when temptation gets real. Whatever you want badly, the devil will present it on a plate before you. When facing such "opportunities," think about what you really want out of life and the people you most love. Reminding yourself of those realities in the heat of the moment may be sufficient to help you overcome. Shift focus from right-now desire to long-term value. Focusing on what and whom you most value makes a major difference.

Facing down temptation is not easy. I am acquainted with nationally prominent pastors whose lapses of morality led to high-profile downfalls. In most cases, these leaders built churches that served their congregations with scriptural, socially relevant teaching and fellowship. Their demise did not mean they were never called to pastor. More than likely, they lost battles with the temptations and demons vexing them.

People often refer to me as a humble man. For what it's worth, one of the best antidotes for temptation is embracing humility focused on who you are at your core. Don't get lost by putting yourself on a pedestal, and don't let others do that to you. You are not the "high-and-mighty, all-wise, most-entitled, reverend-doctor, such-and-such." You are the person God called into full-time ministry; the one who couldn't see how God could use *you* in that way. Hold tight to humility.

When ministry laborers fall, whisper, "But for the grace of God, there go I." Pray for them, and never gloat about your "spotless" record. You are not immune. Let the failures of others motivate you to move closer to God. God is good. He will remove temptations or give you the strength to overcome them, but never forget: without Him, you could be the next headline news for all the wrong reasons.

My father in ministry, Reverend Daniels, instructed me not to talk about pastors' business. He warned against gossiping about my peers to parishioners. "Never bad talk what they've done or build yourself up with favorable comparisons," he said. He taught me to pray for fallen leaders and use their experience as motivation to be more steadfast over my own conduct and decisions. Solid advice.

More Than Just a Habit

Some habits set up leaders for predictable temptations and scandals. Others are benign; however, they fall into the lawful-but-not-helpful bucket noted by Paul:

> *All things are lawful for me, but not all things are helpful; all things are lawful for me, but not all things edify.*
> —1 Corinthians 10:23

Many publications discuss how to address the most-visceral, dangerous habits and the temptations for which they create. For the pastoral audience; however, I prefer to focus on how to address these lawful-but-not-helpful habits because their implications carry more weight for leaders than the average congregant.

Upon accepting God's call, your job is to share the good news of Jesus. As such, regularly assess your relatively non-controversial habits to ensure that exercising them does not conflict with promotion of the gospel.

Consider responsible consumption of alcohol. I find no biblical support for absolute abstinence; however, while I enjoy an occasional glass of wine, I am aware that exercising this habit without restraint could wreak havoc or unleash horrors. Apart from that risk, plenty of people to whom I minister are struggling or reformed alcoholics. Several "mothers of Omega" have lost husbands or children to alcoholism. As such, I generally choose not to indulge in an occasional glass of wine in public. I know prominent pastors who imbibe publicly, but in my opinion, it pays to be mindful of your audience and not confuse those who might be harmed by witnessing your indulgence.

When assessing lawful-but-not-helpful habits, be more concerned about the effect of your actions on others, than on your personal comfort or leisure. Whether an adult beverage, smoking a legal substance or partaking of mainstream—but worldly—forms of entertainment, respect the protective benefits of limiting when and where you indulge. If you cannot strategically abstain, ask the blunt question: Who is my God? Your "lawful" habit may have strayed into stronghold territory.

Be wary of anything that requires you to be a different person—or type of person—to indulge in it. Integrity means that you are the same person regardless of circumstance, not a chameleon who changes depending on the environment. Some of the most painful scandals involved pastors who lived as different people: the Spirit-powered preacher on Sundays, the embezzling fraudster in the church office and the emerging playboy on out-of-town trips.

Stay on your knees before God to avoid this trap. Your spiritual battles should be external, not internal struggles from illicit habits causing you to morph into an unrecognizable shape shifter. Figuring out next steps is difficult enough without warring with multiple spirits and personalities within you. If you feel this happening, don't walk; run to get help. Lean on a few trusted, spiritually-mature family members or mentors who can help you rediscover the Spirit-filled, authentic you God needs.

Protecting Your Morality and Integrity

In *Prayer is Your Fuel* (page 23), I noted how foundational prayer is to a Christian leader. Morality and integrity are extensions of that principle.

A few years into my Omega tenure, I realized just how important prayer was to consistent embracing of my God-given character and personality. I credit a healthy prayer life as the first step to protecting morality and integrity.

No one is immune. Demons are assigned and waiting to take down God's chosen, which is why prayer without ceasing is essential. I confidently guarantee that leaders who sinned against their congregation were forewarned by God. He always speaks.

> *There hath no temptation taken you but such as is common to man: but God is faithful, who will not suffer you to be tempted above that ye are able; but will with the temptation also make a way to escape, that ye may be able to bear it.*
> —1 Corinthians 10:13

God provides an exit strategy in the face of temptation. When He reveals yours, dive through it! God uses military language like "escape" and "warfare" because you are battling with the devil.

Although I may not be the smartest guy in the room, I am one of the more perceptive. I listen for God's voice. Sometimes He speaks to me through strangers talking about something else. In such moments, God tells me to hang onto a specific thought the person shared. Billboards that I passed a thousand times; resound a message about a decision I must make. The Lord speaks to everyone in these subtle ways, if only we listened.

Treasure your mind. Protecting our morality and integrity by weeding habits that cloud your thoughts or dull your perception. You never know when God will send an important message, or exactly how.

Another proactive way to identify instances where morality or integrity may be at risk is asking, "Am I acting as a chaplain inside the empire, or a prophet representing the resistance?" Some are called to minister to the elite, but the vast majority need to focus on—and faithfully represent—the middle class, working class and poor. If everything done pleases community VIPs, your integrity monitoring system should flash red.

I recall an encounter that reminded me of these dynamics. I completed a civil meeting with the CEO of a large healthcare provider that had supported the capital campaign for our Hope Center for Families. As I requested a new donation, the CEO said, "Help me understand how you can ask for our money when you just helped conduct on-site protests of our corporate behavior."

An awkward moment, but not unexpected. Peace flooded me as I said, "I only have one community to represent."

Her corporation had made decisions that were going to cause significant stress and discomfort to many members of my church and the surrounding community. I explained to this executive that at a time when this community was beset by exiting businesses, population loss and reduced tax income, someone had to stand for the people suffering the weight of it. There I sat, minutes after making an earnest pitch for financial support, speaking truth regardless of the consequences. I acknowledged the tough decisions she and her board had to make, but challenged her to lead by making tough choices in the most-humane way. In the end, she did not donate more and I was content with that. You have to decide who you really are, and stand for it. Her company gave a sizeable initial donation, but nothing more. Despite their lack of additional contribution, the center is under construction.

Be prepared for truth-to-power moments. If you work to build community relationships as discussed in the *Walking in Faith Letter* (page 141) while keeping your congregation's needs first, they will come. Consult your daily calendar and pray in advance about encounters, meetings and conferences that will place you at the intersection of the powerful and the needs of those you serve. Thinking ahead enhances your ability to operate with the integrity your congregation and community deserve.

Integrity Pays Off

Being recognized for your integrity is the highest compliment you can receive. Integrity builds on morality. Moral people can be strikingly selfish and mean. Integrity injects fairness and equity into decision-making, and drives you to weigh and balance competing interests and factors. When you live this way, people notice. They may not call when it's time to party, but when they want to get things done—and done well—your phone will ring.

Being a good preacher, or popular pastor, means nothing without integrity. Forming memorable, polished phrases is a nice skill, it's trash if you can't make decisions that combine to a life of purpose and fulfillment.

A difficult aspect of leadership comes when leading with integrity requires you to stand alone. You don't have all the answers or every ounce of practical managerial expertise, but God may lead you in a direction before the rest of the church. In those instances, you have to make tough pronouncements that go against the opinion of your best friend, officers and possibly your spouse. I have faced moments where following God's foresight moved individuals to look at me and say, "Are you crazy?" If people you trust ask that question, pause. Make sure you took time to discern God's voice. If the answer is yes, then stand firm and have courage to follow God.

Early in my tenure at Omega, a decision about the music ministry had to be made. I met with the board and proposed the tough, but necessary decision God placed on my heart. Almost unanimously, the board said, "Yes, pastor. You're right. We need to take that action." Their words were comforting, but their body language spoke volumes. They pushed back from the table and, like Pontius Pilate before the angry mob, "washed their hands" of the situation. I heard the nonverbal message: "Do what you feel led, but bruh, that's on you." It wasn't easy, but I trusted God to make unpopular changes which led to tough conversations. People are not going to agree just because you say that God told you something. They have the right to express conflicting opinions.

The people who most-opposed my music ministry decisions still serve alongside me. Possibly, because of the clue God gave me. Even as they opposed me, amidst the worst of the conflict, God said, "Love them. Keep being their pastor, and don't stop serving them regardless of what they say about you." Despite the temporary organizational turmoil I spurred, I was heartened to see how many people who disagreed—or were personally affected—stuck with me, and the church. Why? Because I refused to let conflict cloud my commitment to their spiritual well-being.

Leading with integrity often involves matters that you cannot disclose to everyone, which may lead to clusters of people whispering about you. In those instances, your job is to love and serve because people are watching you. People take cues from you, so it's critical that you reflect God's love. It's a hard job. That's why you have to be called to succeed at this line of work.

> *Pray for us. We are sure that we have a clear conscience and desire to live honorably in every way.*
> —Hebrews 13:18 NIV

The April 21, 2019 issue of *Dayton Daily News* ran a complimentary front-page story about Vanessa's and my upcoming retirement as co-pastors of Omega. The article featured testimonials from mayors, U.S. congressional representatives, school board leaders and a city commissioner who is my friend and political opponent. The sentiment was not about accomplishments; but rather how Vanessa and I try to live as community leaders. It may seem like no one cares or is paying attention, but when you live for God, people notice and it always pays off.

One of those quoted in the article was Reverend Darryl Fairchild, city commissioner. My relationship with him prospers today because of the mutual integrity exhibited while competing for the same office. Although we entered the race as friends, I was advised to play "hardball" against him in what was predicted to be a close race. While I thought God wanted my next chapter to occur in the political realm, I was uncomfortable taking such advice. I entered debates praying that I did not shame God with my behavior.

Whenever I considered using one of the suggested talking points or attack lines, I couldn't shake the vision of secular voters — or disillusioned Christians — sitting at home nudging one another, saying, "Look at the 'holy' preachers. Give them enough red meat or selfish ambition, and they'll go at it just like the rest of us." I decided that if I had to play like that to win, I would have lost regardless of Election Day results.

My experience running for office raised a question that is healthy for pastors and leaders weighing ambitions and aligning them with God's will: Do you need *everything*? Many spiritual and secular leaders have this mindset, and it seldom leads to a good end. When you work for a greater good, you can look beyond selfish desires to achieve shared success and prosperity that benefits multiple stakeholders. The decision to conduct myself with integrity during my political foray was rewarded. While I lost the battle, I was blessed with greater clarity about the next phase of my ministry.

The closer you walk with God, the more you appreciate the rewards that come with morality and integrity. The rewards are rarely immediate and not always quantifiable. The payoff may come in quality relationships with your congregants rather than the quantity of worshippers or value of tithes and offerings. While it takes true faith to appreciate these benefits and work to protect your morality and integrity, I raise my hand as a witness that it's absolutely worth the effort.

Daryl Ward

Letter 10

Walking in Faith

Principle:
The cultivation and exercise of your faith will be critical in many ways. Whether charting the course of your church's ministries and programs, managing personal finances or discerning if God is calling you into a new phase of ministry, let your actions be faith-based. Strengthen your faith foundation by walking with God daily as He incrementally steers you along your ministry path.

Dear Son,

I walked a dynamic, diverse path throughout my ministry career. Some transitions and challenges were more difficult than others, and I saw bright and dreary days. Even in the darkest nights, I believed God had a larger plan operating, even if I couldn't see it. That is the definition of faith.

It helps that I continually witnessed that God never wastes anything. As I shared in the *Time Management Letter* (page 117), the purpose of many experiences are not revealed until months or years later. Even when I was critically ill, I believed God had a plan for my health crisis. I was not certain that the plan included earthly healing (He uses death in incredible ways), but I reflected on one of Prophet Jeremiah's most-quoted verses:

> *"For I know the thoughts that I think toward you,"*
> *says the Lord, "thoughts of peace and not of evil, to*
> *give you a future and a hope."*
> —Jeremiah 29:11

Applying faith can transform your effectiveness in ministry and provide a foundation that sustains you through the inevitable ups-and-downs that come with pastoring a church. I hope to prod the way you think about faith by discussing it in three distinct contexts:

- Equipping yourself for ministry without trusting your capabilities over God's
- Exercising faith in personal finance
- Transitioning to a new, God-appointed assignment

As important as these three examples are, it helps to start with a story illustrating the faith that should motivate every minister of the gospel.

An Unpredictable Harvest: The Power of Faithful Ministry

It is healthy for ambitious ministers, pastors and leaders to pull back and reflect from the perspective of those who could be served by our ministries. Transformations in society can be a little intimidating. For example, millennials are looking for a worship experience that differs noticeably from the preferences of their parents and grandparents. Adapting to generational transitions is complicated by challenges inherent to operating a ministry located in economically-stressed and disadvantaged communities.

Consider how irrelevant the average church may appear to a youth born into a low-income, high-crime environment where no one owns a home and responsible parents are an anomaly. When I think about how to reach children or young adults from such areas, I attempt to imagine the extreme, as I put myself in their shoes.

Try it: What if you were reared in the figurative "wild" like Tarzan? What if all you knew was an environment rife with violence? A place where you ate raw food and walked on all fours. Where everyone smoked dope, abused alcohol—and their sexual partners—and cursed like sailors. The Tarzan metaphor may seem extreme, but I use it to signify the extent to which such environments deteriorate with each passing generation.

This environment is the one to which God may call you. Some pastors and their churches spend more time "in the jungle" than others, but every ministry should have a presence in such communities. When you think of the situations into which these youth were born, you realize the only way to help is to walk into their midst and pull them into the light of Christ's love.

A legendary seminary dean told me the origin story of his faith walk. It began with his father, an orphan and foster child, who was reared in a brothel. The dean's father told him of a time when he stood outside, cleaning liquor bottles discarded by the prostitutes' clientele. A group of men walked by, ministered to him about their local church. Instead of a one-and-done visit; they visited him weekly, building a relationship that drew him to accept Christ and join the church. Those men rescued him from a toxic environment.

This man went on to build a respectable career, get married and raise three sons, but the investment those Christian men made in him does not end there. Not only did his son spend forty years leading a seminary that produced countless influential pastors, his other sons became a bishop and a pastor who birthed three mega-churches.

When I think of the pastor who commissioned (or perhaps, personally led) the men who pulled this future father out of "the wild" and into the marvelous light, I can only say, "Look at God!" This church is called to take faith-based action to the most-challenging environments and find at-risk people. You will not live long enough to see these generational harvests fulfilled, but rest easy knowing that God will get the glory.

Your Capabilities or God's: Faith Means Knowing Whose Matters More

God likely used my knowledge of this story to inspire a faith step that significantly expanded the scope of Omega's ministry.

About eighteen months after my health crisis, I had regained the ability to walk but did not consider myself fully healed. I preached more and was visible Sundays to assure the congregation that I could continue as pastor, but my mind was not running at full speed. As I delegated responsibilities to Vanessa and my ministerial staff, I asked God what I should do with my spare time.

In the preceding months, while undergoing physical therapy and regaining basic motor skills, I was in regular prayer about the conditions of some of the worst parts of the city. As I sought God about who could stand in the gap in our most-challenged, West Dayton communities and neighborhoods surrounding Omega Church, I heard God's challenge. "The most visible people are the pimps and drug dealers. Where is the church? Pastors should reclaim those streets."

I pushed to recruit Christian men to walk with me through these violent parts of our city. As weeks passed, pastors from the inner city and far-flung suburbs walked with me. Our walks, which usually culminated in a rally where clergy and community activists spoke, were a great success for a time. Not only did we conduct periodic "feel good" events, we established new connections between churches, activists and the people likely to commit violent acts or fall victim to them. These results reminded me never give up on God. The Lord often shows up when situations look the most desolate. I love this translation of Lamentations:

> *When life is heavy and hard to take, go off by yourself, enter the silence. Bow in prayer. Don't ask questions: Wait for hope to appear. Don't run from trouble. Take it full-face. The "worst" is never the worst.*
> —Lamentations 3:29 The Message

The positive attention generated by the community walks led two local civic leaders to invite Omega to participate in an experimental city and county program called the Community Initiative to Reduce Gun Violence, or CIRGV. CIRGV partners with local law enforcement to provide life-changing supportive services to individuals wanting positive transformation, and engages the community to promote a neighborhood standard that openly values life and safety while denouncing gun violence. I was asked to work with CIRGV to help hire and place "street advocates" who intercede in high-crime areas. Equipped with safety measures including bulletproof vests, these courageous, peaceful individuals daily go into neighborhoods seeking opportunities to defuse conflicts and disrupt stubborn cycles of vengeance.

This innovative program was in an embryonic stage, so I imagine the civic leaders needed someone who was crazy enough to try it. I am so grateful they asked me to participate. The CIRGV program, which started in 2008 continues today and is hailed as a success by community groups, churches and law enforcement. In an average year, the CIRGV advocates commissioned by Omega's Community Development Corporation (CDC) help de-escalate 200 potentially violent situations. CIRGV was the CDC's first fully-funded program. It has been the foundation for our Hope Center for Families and other programs we have in area schools and organizations. After more than ten years of serving the community, CIRGV is set to conclude September 2019.

> *Now to Him who is able to do immeasurably more than all we ask or imagine, according to His power that is at work within us.*
> —Ephesians 3:20 NIV

God's ability to get results is a clear example for me. When I followed His nudge to walk in troubled places even while in "recovery mode," I walked in faith without seeing these coming developments.

This episode reminds me of the power of walking in faith and drives home that God's capabilities will power my ministry far more than anything I contribute.

Another example is my somewhat rare status as a traditionally credentialed pastor who holds a reputable law degree.

My multi-faceted background may have impressed a few potential Omega members and bought some early credibility with local officials and dignitaries. Looking back; however, I know ministry accomplishments had little to do with my legal acumen. When Omega was part of a high-profile community development initiative, I applied every bit of my legal knowledge to protect our rights. I was proud of the work I did to insist on protective contract language, but the joke was on me. Despite my efforts, most of the partnerships deteriorated and Omega backed out of the initiative.

I took a lesson from that experience. From the purchase of the Harvard Campus through its ongoing development, I have not approached related administrative and contractual matters like a lawyer. God showed me how to focus on being the best pastor and community servant possible. I trust Him, and the legal resources to which He guides us, with the rest. I am grateful for my legal education, but I view it with proper perspective. Don't put stock in personal capabilities and worldly knowledge over God's wisdom and insight. Invest in capabilities and knowledge that can benefit you and your church, but remember that God can work through you despite your lack of knowledge or capability.

Faith and Your Finances

No matter how Holy-Spirit filled you are, managing personal finances can test the limits of your faith. Year after year, surveys indicate that financial management is the leading cause of divorce. If the temptation and tough choices embedded in finances can destroy marriages, they can obstruct your ability to pastor and lead with maximum clarity and power.

To combat this inherent risk, pray about how to avoid letting the cost of your wardrobe, car or house distract from your ministry. God will help you develop your own monitoring system. Give Him your unique, individual styles and preferences and He will help you manage them without giving up all of them. I saw God develop this self-monitoring system by exposing me to two nationally pre-eminent pastors. As I worked with Jeremiah Wright and Johnny Ray Youngblood, I noted with surprise that neither was the "snappy dresser" I had assumed. That reinforced my decision to take a humble approach to my style and manner of dress.

When I sought God for guidance on what to value and where to indulge desires, instead of the fancy house or expensive car, my greatest satisfaction came from the basics:

- Healthy and happy children
- A beautiful wife and "help meet" who helped me pursue God's ongoing call
- Memorable family vacations

Pursuing God's call resulted in work that I would have done without pay. When it hit me as a rare privilege, it made sense to tamp down my desires for "the finer things."

The best way to keep your finances in control is to remember that you work for God.

Delight thyself also in the Lord: and He shall give thee the desires of thine heart.
—Psalm 37:4

Meditate on Psalm 37, especially verse 4, as you ask Him to give you "the desires of your heart." When you sincerely seek God, you will have new appreciation for the ways in which He keeps His promises and provides for you. I am not saying that He called you to a life of poverty because that takes a special anointing. God's grace is far more generous and overflowing than you can imagine. Trust Him.

Financial Faith in Action
In 2009, as Dayton's economy weathered the fallout of the nation's historic economic crisis, Omega took a direct hit. Offerings were down significantly, the balance sheet was in bad shape, and the board took bold steps to stop the bleeding. Not only did this action require laying off or furloughing several staff; the board came for me. My salary was nearly cut in half.

No point sugar coating my reaction: I panicked! I didn't see how my family could manage, if I did not land a second job to replace the lost income. I talked to "important" friends whom I assumed could help me land such a gig. I contacted presidents of several universities, not knowing what to ask, but seeking a way to earn an extra check.

Two things happened. First, my initial outreach yielded little in terms of the perfect side gig. Then, God spoke to me. "Trust Me," He whispered again and again. While in the throes of panic, I missed His gentle reminder. As His message settled, peace fell on me. I focused on working with Vanessa to downsize our budget.

As I assess those fraught days with the benefit of hindsight, I was better equipped than many to handle the drastic income reduction. We had helped our grown children cover the costs of undergraduate schooling. As a result, our mandatory expenses decreased noticeably. I didn't require the income needed a few years earlier. God's timing is perfect.

Self-examination revealed that the years I earned the most money were the same ones in which I felt poorest. My spending priorities were unbalanced and I often lacked cash to buy a cup of coffee. A true low point because I wasted money and deprivation of coffee feels like a crisis! As the clouds lifted and my financial vision cleared, I realized the importance of trusting God with my money.

In the years since that infamous pay cut, God provided me with the finances to do everything I needed to do. We don't live extravagantly, but by appreciating what we have, it's not burdensome to take Vanessa out for nice meals and enjoyable dates. I don't know how God orders our finances, but we can unleash His mercy by taking financial burdens to Him, and leaving them there.

When you ask Him to help you focus—and spend—on what matters, you can achieve financial freedom that matches your income to your authentic needs and God-given desires.

The Power of a Mustard Seed: Reaping the Benefits of Faith

> *He replied, "Because you have so little faith. Truly I tell you, if you have faith as small as a mustard seed, you can say to this mountain, 'Move from here to there,' and it will move. Nothing will be impossible for you."*
> —Matthew 17:20 NIV

Just a small quantity of faith, spread across every area of your life makes all the difference in the efficacy of your ministry. Because faith undergirds every dimension of Christian leadership, its benefits are far-reaching. Hopefully, the two applications presented—consistent awareness that God's capabilities must always trump yours, and conscious aligning of your financial management with God-given desires—are sufficiently visceral illustrations.

Daryl Ward

Letter 11

Transitions:

Knowing When It's Time to Go & Why

Principle:
Although you don't know how many church moves or directional changes will be part of your ministry path, you can follow daily principles that help smooth these inevitable transitions. By focusing on the needs of your present church and community, tuning into God's voice and holding ministry plans loosely, you maximize the ability to sense coming transitions and increase the likelihood that when you exit, the ministry left behind continues to thrive.

Dear Son,

The pastor I succeeded at Omega served until the age of 96. He died on duty; having preached the morning's message, he sat and collapsed. It was common for pastors to die "with their preaching boots on." Many Black preachers had no choice but to do so; with few congregations funding insurance policies and pensions. To keep money coming in, my predecessors sacrificed the luxury of retirement. Fortunately, growth of the Black middle class—along with increased compensation expectations of educated pastors—drove more churches to protect their leaders' financial security with competitive benefit and retirement plans.

While these developments free pastors from clinging to their churches like life preservers, they sometimes complicate decisions regarding when it's time to retire or move to a new ministry. In *Partnering with Your Spouse Letter* (page 87), I discussed communing with God to discern your unique ministry path. Conventional wisdom that engulfs you—whether bias toward staying with a church for decades or hopping from one church to a larger one—can cloud your judgment. Focus on the following items before worrying about whether God is calling you to a new church:

1. Commit to stay long enough to build relationships that power successful ministries.

    God seldom moves through pastors and leaders who did not first build deep, trusting relationships with their congregations and communities. Lasting change occurs through the power of relationships built on mutual trust and respect. The reputation you and your church develop will open ministry opportunities and, most importantly, open hearts to the gospel. While reputations are so fragile that a single act can ruin them, they cannot be developed overnight. They require years of faithful actions that match your words.

    Although I am a Baptist minister, I have admired pastors from the Methodist church. While Methodists generally operate an itinerant system in which pastors rotate from church-to-church, successful pastors with whom I am acquainted put down long-term roots in one place. Floyd Flake of Greater Allen AME Cathedral in Jamaica Queens, New York, and Mike Slaughter of Ginghamsburg Church in Tipp City, Ohio spring to mind. I am aware of pastors who moved routinely with success at one church after another; however, they are rare. Depending on the denomination and church structure, you have limited control over how long you pastor at any given church. However, as long as God has you there, build deep, trusting relationships as a strategic act of faith. The quality of these relationships transformed Omega's ministry. The same relationships transformed me into the leader the church needed.

2. Build a sustainable infrastructure that will survive your tenure.
   For young pastors, it probably sounds dramatic to urge that you not let your church die with you. Think of it this way: Do you love your congregation enough to leave it in good condition when God calls you to pastor a larger, more-influential ministry? If so, it is important to get about the business of building a sustainable infrastructure that empowers your successor. Assess your church's leadership team, operating processes and community presence. Compare your observations to the structures and processes in place at peer churches you admire. Where are gaps and shortfalls? How can they be addressed in the coming year?

Be serious about developing capabilities that are lacking or may leave the church exposed from financial, operational or serving perspectives. Improving your operational structure and underlying processes can improve how everyone works together, generate greater collaboration and produce measurable results. This type of work often requires maturity to forego resources and devote them to future endeavors.

You may have to confront individuals who have personal benefit to you, but harm the church. The difficulty and controversies may tempt you to lay this work aside, but war against that temptation by considering if you love your church enough to equip it for a future that may not include you. When you leave, manage your exit allowing the church to send you off with a great party, not a funeral.

3. Innovate by looking "up the road."

   Leaders should always look up the road, discerning present and budding needs of the community and equipping the church accordingly. Early in my Omega tenure, I sensed I needed assistance developing this type of foresight. Desiring someone who could help drive innovation and bring future-focused energy, I hired a bright, young assistant, Harry L. White, Jr. He has since gone on to pastor Watts Chapel Missionary Baptist Church in Raleigh, North Carolina. Harry often reminded me to factor in feedback and input from multiple constituencies when making decisions about Omega's direction. As he noted, most of our members were ten years older or ten years younger than me. God called me to make the decisions, but I needed multiple perspectives to assess where our ministries should head.

Another aspect of finding sources of innovation came from marrying faith with available examples of His work. Vanessa and I might have missed God's call to purchase and develop the expanded campus if we limited the "possible" to ministries in the vicinity. As our vision to directly address residents' medical, mental health, educational and safety needs took shape, it seldom resembled what other Dayton-area churches did.

We drew on interactions with inspiring leaders like Kevin Cosby, Walter Malone, Alvin O'Neal Jackson, Otis Moss Jr., Mike Slaughter, Floyd Flake and Johnny Ray Youngblood. These men lead churches that developed programs delivering affordable housing, schooling and healthcare to their congregations and nearby residents. While few have accomplished what they have, their experience proved that any vision from God can be achieved.

These pastors, and many more, gave us the fortitude to innovate. Those innovations produced outstanding successes like Omega School of Excellence, which equipped hundreds of students who are promising, productive members of society. Looking up the road does not guarantee success in every instance, but it provides you with the opportunity to position the church for growth and greater effect on those God called the congregation to serve.

4. Put the needs of your church before your own.

As I aged, my ability to deliver a bracing-and-relevant Word for millennial and college-aged members waned. Sensing when it is time to leave your present post is about staying prayerful. The signs rarely hit you all at once like Saul's Damascus-Road experience.

A few years ago, I illustrated a point in a sermon with lighthearted assurance that I would voluntarily retire long before my congregation tired of me. My promise drew good-natured laughter; however, I was sincere. Throughout my experiences as pastor and seminary administrator, I realized that God journeyed with me through a variety of callings and missions. From the day I accepted His call, He remained the same whether He called me to preach, pastor, educate or serve in the streets. I learned to keep walking with Him and trust the path He led me down, one step and one corner at a time. That's why I hold loosely to specific trappings and blessings of pastoring. Simply put, I learned not to get drunk on "amens."

That mindset allowed me to process new developments. After several challenging years, the Omega Community Development Corporation (CDC) started to hit its stride in launching initiatives to develop the expanded campus. Vanessa served as head of the CDC and the administrative demands consumed all of her time. I performed the bulk of weekly preaching and church administration, but was aware that for every long-term Omega member who connected with my preaching style and messages, new worshippers responded more to messages delivered by younger associate ministers including Joshua.

My son faithfully served the church for over a decade as youth pastor and then assistant to the pastors. He added a M.Div. degree to the law degree he earned after graduation from Morehouse College. On the Sundays he preached, I was struck by the extent to which God gifted him with a fresh Word. His style, illustrations and transparency about life application animated worshippers of every age.

It took time, but I came to see that God was preparing Omega for a new era. Vanessa made great progress developing the expanded campus, but we agreed that she could benefit from an executive assistant. We developed a dynamic corps of associate ministers who lead children and teens throughout the city, and managed the Urban Leadership Academy, which equipped lay ministers from congregations across the region. In addition to the church's success, God equipped Joshua to pastor "somebody's church."

God gives resources for a reason. When you see them developing, communicate with Him about what that reason is. I knew God gave us these resources because He wanted more work done on His behalf. As I sought Him about it, He called me toward territory I could never explore as a full-time pastor: the challenge of establishing strategic, long-term collaboration between the church and the community. Omega tasted success in this arena on a small, intermittent scale; however, the stirring in my spirit indicated we could do this on a larger scale by establishing a place for spiritual leadership where people across denominations could make a difference to the most-embattled citizens.

The pull of the call let me know that it was time to prepare to leave my pastoral post. This pull necessitated a series of frank discussions with Omega's leadership. Vanessa and I informed the board of our vision regarding respective roles. That news required development of an orderly, democratic process that produced Omega's new senior pastor. Though I believed Joshua was called to that responsibility, I removed myself from the deliberations. As Dean Newell Wert taught, "trust the process" when developing associate ministers. That experience helped me focus on my role in the transition as the board and congregation assessed Joshua as my successor. Far from an overnight sensation, my son was voted pastor-elect after nearly twelve years of service.

Stepping aside empowered Omega to minister in a more-contemporary fashion on Sundays, and freed me to venture into the community as its advocate and bridge-builder for the services we hope to perform at the expanded campus.

My challenge is that I stepped into another faith-testing season of my ministry path.

5. Be flexible: Your calling today may be different tomorrow.

As my retirement nears, it's not uncommon for congregants to express mixed emotions. A person raves about Joshua's preaching and overall development as a leader before asking a version of

"Do you really have to leave us so soon?" I get it. While most Baptist pastors transition into "emeritus" status, I am doing so younger than most, with all my faculties and abilities intact.

This fact made my decision easier. Serving as pastor is the safe, straightforward path. I have a wealth of experience at pastoring, so I know where the alarms, land mines and controls levers are. Had I not fully recovered from my debilitating health crisis, I might be tempted to "ride out" my senior years doing what comes natural.

Instead, I signed up for a new, developing phase of ministry that bursts with possibility and seeded with plenty of opportunities for failure. Divining this new path will involve false starts. After announcing my retirement and initiating evaluating Joshua as successor, I experimented with a foray into politics. I considered running for office years earlier. As I mulled next steps, I sensed that public service might allow me to foster collaboration between local government and faith-based institutions.

After praying and weighing opportunities, I ran for a seat on Dayton's city commission. The ensuing election campaign taught me lots about the political realm including that I don't care for many aspects of it. I lost a close race, but the outcome was the best one possible. God didn't embarrass me, but moved to protect me. The responsibilities of an elected office would have forced ongoing clashes between my leadership style and the political arena. I would not have time to develop new insights I received about how to accelerate realization of our shared vision for the expanded campus. Steering clear of conflicts of interest might have limited my ability to participate in much of this important work.

Sometimes walking with God is like being in a maze with a friend who has the map. God doesn't show you the full path, or even long stretches of it, at once. He asks you to follow His directions, one-step at a time. If He shared any more than that, would you say, "I'll take it from here"? While trusting in your abilities, you would miss the maturation process crafted to have you positioned to serve upon arrival.

The future is more exciting when you trust God instead of doing the predictable, safe things. I am excited to take on the challenges inherent in the next season of ministry. I will work to accelerate fund raising for Hope Center and other community service initiatives, and establish a continuing education program to equip area residents with critical life skills, professional expertise and ministry capabilities. Many churches are trapped in tradition, and are not exploring ways to minister to people that hit them where they live. The work of Omega CDC can help churches and other faith-based organizations increase their relevance for those they serve.

An added bonus is I don't have to give up preaching to do this work. While I don't envision myself crisscrossing the country, I will accept preaching invitations from near and far. I can use guest appearances at churches and organizations to expand CDC's network. Where some might ask how I can give up all that comes with being a pastor, I am excited by the prospect of the new things that I can do.

I embrace this new season as "spiritual entrepreneurship" as I match my actions with faith that God will deliver what He promised. When God places a ministry vision on your heart, accepting it means putting yourself in places waiting to be served. Unless you are willing to step out on faith and enter those places, the vision will never materialize.

Flexibility becomes vital as you discern each twist and turn while working out of your ministry. Other than experience, I have no proof that this next phase will be a stunning success. The possibility exists that Vanessa and I may never see the campus achieve the vision God called us to lead the church to pursue so many years ago. Even if nothing pans out according to our hopes, I know that I have been true to His voice and challenge. I don't have all the answers, but I know God wants leaders who will faithfully follow Him. As you feel Him lay visions on your heart, do what He says and let Him work out the rest.

To ensure your flexibility and maximize your ability to heed His guidance through ministry transitions, I have specific suggestions:

- Never let yourself get too comfortable or wedded to the trappings or luxuries of your current ministry role. When you refuse to cling to privileges of pastoring a large church, for example, you stay more tuned to God's nudges because you won't automatically rule out the "still, small voice" that suggests you give them up. Make sure you focus on your relationship with Him above all else. He has a path for you, and He will communicate it to you.

- Take regular time by yourself to seek God's wisdom and guidance. Ask Him to help you live a life that pleases Him. When you live with that as your primary goal, your ministry path will never stale. That God-focused life makes for a journey in which there's always work to do, as God—who doesn't waste anything—uses your prior ministry experience to equip you for the next mission.

Transitions Will Always Be on the Table: Be Ready

When you build ministries powered by strong relationships, invest in sustainable infrastructures that could survive your tenure, keep an eye on how to innovate and put your church's needs before your own, people will notice. While following these principles will prepare you to deal with potential and divinely-inspired periods of transition, they may ironically result in opportunities to leave your present post.

You will confront developments—some externally-generated, others bubble from a stirring within—that will raise the possibility that it is time to move to a new church or ministry. Since these developments are inevitable, why not live and lead now to make them easier to manage? I tried to "practice what I preach," and this prescription is true. I thank God for how He rewarded my faith with a new phase of ministry that is as unpredictable and daunting as it is exciting and potentially ground-breaking. A post I saw on Facebook sums it up so well:

"I trust the next chapter because I know the Author."

Daryl Ward

Closing Thoughts

Thank you for reading the ways my journey might help you trust God throughout your own. My pastoral career brought accolades, awesome relationships and a front-row seat to the many ways God can work in the lives of His children. There have been challenges and trials throughout, but I appreciate the blessings that sustained me. I don't have my parents anymore; however, in addition to a loyal, beautiful and brilliant wife I have three incredible children and four magnificent grandchildren. God has been gracious to me.

Yet somehow, I yearn for more.

I long for more uniquely thrilling moments that occur when you witness the hatching of God's vision for His people. I love the patient labor of serving as a midwife for His vision in my church and my community. As I anticipate this new season of ministry, the vision is God's, not mine and I await the details.

In the meantime, as Vanessa's and my partnership shifts to the Omega Community Development Corporation, I can first contribute with operational and administrative tasks like following up on projects that I could not give proper attention.

I specialize in digging around dark recesses, seeking that first glimmer of light that reveals a radiant glow in the distance. The journey does not intimidate me because I love making the inevitable missteps as the light intensifies. I love the God who protects me and transforms those missteps into miracles that facilitate the saving of souls by meeting people where they are, and addressing their spiritual and earthly needs.

I faced similar when a vision manifested. I felt tempted to pause and polish trophies or pat myself on the back for newly notched victories. Instead, I keep an ear to the ground, sensing the rumblings that answer the question "What's next?"

Through every letter, I encouraged you to pray. I close this book doing what I urged you to do. I am praying and waiting on God; doing my best to quiet the noise so I can hear when He beckons.

To Joshua and you reading this book, don't let questions of what I or other veteran pastors did limit your perception of what God might call or equip you to do. Don't shrink from visions that challenge you to tackle things from which others shrank. Don't be afraid to fail. I learned much more from the failures than the unearned successes.

You are now the pastor. Embrace this reality. Pray and seek grand visions, but while the vision materializes, work on that next "right thing" that is in tune with God's will. Keep at it, and before you know it, it will be your time to retire! As with most privileged experiences, your service in full-time ministry will feel fleeting so enjoy the ride.

I pray this passage motivates you with the same power it gives me:

> *Not that I am speaking of being in need, for I have learned in whatever situation I am to be content. I know how to be brought low, and I know how to abound. In any and every circumstance, I have learned the secret of facing plenty and hunger, abundance and need. I can do all things through Him who strengthens me.*
> —Philippians 4:11-13 ESV

Paul started with his partnership with the Philippians, then shifted focus to his partnership with God. My partnership with God benefits from faith that is not determined by circumstances. Circumstance-driven faith can falter in need ("Why hasn't God provided for me?") or plenty ("Look at what I have accomplished").

Never question God's power to accomplish anything through your ministry. Do you have the courage and conviction to humbly see each task, trial and effort through to completion?

I encourage you to hold daily to the inspirational promise of verse 13, while letting verses 11-12 remind you of the prerequisite to doing "all things." Walk faithfully through the journey God assigns you, appreciating His love, protection and provision.

Daryl Ward

Letters to My Son

About Reverend Daryl Ward

As a nationally recognized pastor and seminarian, Daryl Ward speaks to the needs of the un-churched and at-risk urban communities. With innovative programming, he and his wife, Co-Pastor Vanessa, led Omega Baptist Church in Dayton, OH to embrace its "church unusual" identity.

Reverend Ward served as senior pastor from 1988 through 2019. During his thirty years of service, the ministry grew from 100 to 4,000 members at its peak.

A graduate of Georgetown University Law Center and Colgate Rochester Divinity School, Reverend Ward served as director of admissions, dean of African-American Ministries and president and chief operating officer of United Theological Seminary.

His awards and recognitions include
- Honorary doctorate from Simmons Bible College
- Honorary chief of Ekumfi Asokwa Village in Ghana, West Africa
- Distinguished Alumni Award from Colgate Rochester Divinity School

The Wards are the proud parents of three children and four grandchildren.

Dr. Ward is available to speak to your school, church or organization. Whether a ten-minute presentation or a full-day workshop, this expert will encourage, inspire and empower your group to execute ministry excellence! For inquiries about speaking engagements and bulk book purchases, visit DarylWard.org or email darylward01@gmail.com.

About Chet Kelly Robinson

Chet Kelly Robinson is the author of seven commercially-published novels including the #1 best-selling *No More Mr. Nice Guy* and critically acclaimed, *Between Brothers* (Random House). His books—which have been selected as favorite reads by dozens of national book clubs—received favorable reviews in publications including *Publishers Weekly, Essence, Washington Post* and *Chicago Sun-Times*.

Chet, his wife and two children are active and appreciative members of Omega Baptist Church. Connect with Chet at LinkedIn.com/in/ChetKRobinson.

About Queen V Publishing

The Doorway to

YOUR Destiny!

Go thou and publish abroad the kingdom of God.
—Luke 9:60 ESV

Committed to transforming manuscripts into polished works of art, **Queen V Publishing** is a company of standard and integrity. We offer an alternative that allows the message in YOU to do what it was sent to do for OTHERS.

QueenVPublishing.com

Serving professional speakers and experts to magnify and monetize their message by publishing quality books

www.ingramcontent.com/pod-product-compliance
Lightning Source LLC
Chambersburg PA
CBHW070601010526
44118CB00012B/1417